D0105421

Valdosta Church of Christ

12/84

Straight Talk to

MEN

and Their Wives

Other books by Dr. James C. Dobson

Dr. James C. Dobson

Straight Talk to
MEN
and Their Wives

WORD BOOKS
PUBLISHER
WACO, TEXAS

Scripture quotations marked NIV from The Holy Bible, New International Version, copyright © 1978 by New York International Bible Society. Scripture quotation marked PHILLIPS from The New Testament in Modern English, copyright 1958, 1959, 1960 by J. B. Phillips; used by permission of the Macmillan Company. Scripture quotations marked TLB from The Living Bible, Paraphrased (Wheaton: Tyndale House Publishers, 1971) and used by permission. Scripture quotations marked RSV from the Revised Standard Version of the Bible, copyrighted 1946, 1952, © 1971, 1973 by the Division of Christian Education of the National Council of the Churches of Christ in the U.S.A., and used by permission.

ISBN 0–8499–0260–6
Library of Congress catalog card number: 80–51595
Printed in the United States of America

Illustrations by Dennis Bellile

First printing, May 1980
Second printing, September 1980
Third printing, December 1980
Fourth printing, March 1981
Fifth printing, November 1981
Sixth printing, December 1981
Seventh printing, June 1982
Eighth Printing, November 1982
Ninth Printing, May 1983

This book is affectionately dedicated to the memory of my father, James Dobson, Sr., for reasons which will be understood as these pages are read.

Contents

SECTION I

WHAT IS A MAN?

Chapter 1

My Father

WHO COULD have suspected on such a pleasant afternoon that my father, at sixty-six years of age, was enjoying his final moments on this earth? He held the baby and chatted amiably with members of the family. A Sunday dinner was then placed on the table and Dad was asked to bless the food. This good man, James Dobson, Sr., bowed his head one last time and thanked the Lord for his generosity and love. It was to be his own benediction, for, minutes later, God beckoned his soul across the chilly waters of death. There was no struggle, no pain, no agonizing "goodbyes." He simply paused, then leaned toward my mother and was gone.

An hour later, my wife reached me by telephone to break the news. I was speaking twelve hundred miles to the west, and had devoted my remarks that day to the importance of Christian

11

fatherhood. In fact, I talked throughout the morning about my dad and the beautiful example he had set before me. Then came Shirley's call. We shared an incredible sense of grief and loss in that moment. Only those who "have been there" will fully comprehend such an experience.

The funeral was held three days later, at which time I delivered a tribute to my father. Somehow I managed to express the following words from my heart on that cold December day.

The Tribute

To our friends and loved ones, I want to express appreciation on behalf of our family for each of you being here today. We appreciate your coming to honor the man whom we loved so dearly—the man whose name I share.

I asked my mother for this privilege of paying tribute to my dad, although quite honestly, this is the most difficult moment of my life. This man whose body lies before me was not only my father and my friend, but he was also the source of great inspiration for me. Few people realize that most of my writings are actually an expression of his views and his teachings. Whenever we were together, he would talk and I usually took notes. That's the kind of relationship we had, and his loss is devastating to me.

So I don't apologize for the grief that overwhelms me in this hour. These are not tears of guilt or remorse or regret. I have no bitter memories . . . there were no harsh words that I wish I could retrieve . . . we had no conflicts or struggles or strife. The emotion that you see reflects only the love of a son who has suddenly lost his father and gentle friend.

Some of you are aware that my dad had a very serious heart attack in September of this year. Shirley and I had traveled to San Antonio, Texas, where I was to speak to the Texas Pediatric Society on Friday. When we arrived at the hotel on Thursday night, we received a message from Dr. Paul Cunningham, indicating that my dad was in intensive care in a Kansas City hospital. On Friday morning, Dr. Cunningham called again to say that my father's condition had worsened and he was not expected to live through the night. He also informed me that my uncle, Dr. James McGraw, had died in the same hospital at 10:30 that morning. It is impossible to describe the sorrow that Shirley and I felt as we flew to Kansas City that afternoon. We never expected to see my dad alive again and went through all the agonies of his loss. But when we arrived at the airport, we learned that my dad had made a remarkable improvement and was anticipating our visit at the hospital. How thankful I will always be that God answered our prayers and granted us seventy-nine more days—beautiful, golden days—before He took my dad to heaven on December 4, 1977.

May I share with you what thoughts went through my troubled mind on that endless plane trip from San Antonio to Kansas City? I journeyed backward in time, experiencing a kaleidoscope of early memories. I thought about the very happiest days of my life, occurring when I was between ten and thirteen years of age. My dad and I would arise very early before the sun came up on a wintry morning. We would put on our hunting clothes and heavy boots, and drive twenty miles from the little town where we lived. After parking the car and climbing over a fence, we entered a wooded area which I called the "big woods" because the trees seemed so large to me. We would slip down to the creek bed and follow that winding stream several miles back into the forest.

Then my dad would hide me under a fallen tree which made a little room with its branches. He would find a similar shelter for himself around a bend in the creek. Then we would await the arrival of the sun and the awakening of the animal world. Little squirrels and birds and chipmunks would scurry back and forth, not knowing they were being observed. My dad and I then watched as the breathtaking panorama of the morning unfolded, which spoke so eloquently of the God who made all things.

But most importantly, there was something dramatic that occurred out there in the forest between my dad and me. An intense love and affection was generated on those mornings that set the tone for a lifetime of fellowship. There was a closeness and a oneness that made me want to be like that man . . . that made me choose his values as my values, his dreams as my dreams, his God as my God.

These were among the memories that surged through my mind on that lonely plane trip in September. Then another flood of emotion came over me, as I thought about my own children. I wondered what memories will predominate in their minds when I lie at the point of death, a moment or two from now. What will they remember to be the happiest experiences of their lives? Will they recall a busy father who was preoccupied with writing books and catching planes and answering mail and talking on the telephone and being a "big man"? Or will they recall a patient dad who took time to love them and teach them and enjoy the beauty of God's world with them? I pray that the Lord will help me keep my little family at the top of my list of priorities during the precious prime-time years.

James Dobson was a man of many intense loves. His greatest passion was expressed in his love for Jesus Christ. His every thought and deed were motivated or influenced by his desire to serve his Lord. And I can truthfully say that we were never together without my being drawn closer to God by being in his presence. Not because he warned me or chastised me . . . but because his love for the Lord penetrated and shaped my own attitudes.

The last conversation I ever held with my dad reflected my confidence in his faith. Exactly five days before his death, I telephoned him from Los Angeles at 11:27 A.M.

I said, "Dad, I have an appointment at 11:30 and can only talk for three minutes. I am calling because I face some decisions this afternoon which are very important to me professionally, and I want you to pray for me." His final words were, "I *will* pray about it, Jim." You can be sure that he did!

My dad also loved my mother with great intensity. This fact was beautifully illustrated last year when my parents came to visit us in California. Dad and I took a walk in a nearby park one morning, and as usual, he was talking and I was writing. He then reached into his pocket and retrieved a crumpled sheet of paper which looked very old.

He said, "You might be interested in reading this statement. These are words I expressed to your mother before we were married, forty-two years ago. They were not read to her, but I later wrote down the thoughts I had communicated."

This message was written on the paper.

I want you to understand and be fully aware of my feelings concerning the marriage covenant which we are about to enter. I have been taught at my mother's knee, and in harmony with the Word of God, that the marriage vows are inviolable, and by entering into them, I am binding myself absolutely and for life. The idea of estrangement from you through divorce for any reason at all (although God allows one—infidelity) will never at any time be permitted to enter into my thinking. I'm not naïve in this. On the contrary, I'm fully aware of the possibility, unlikely as it now appears, that mutual incompatibility or other unforeseen circumstances, could result in extreme mental suffering. If such becomes the case, I am resolved for my part to accept it as a consequence of the commitment I am now making, and to bear it, if necessary, to the end of our lives together.

I have loved you dearly as a sweetheart and will continue to love you as my wife. But over and above that, I love you with a Christian love that demands that I never react in any way toward you that would jeopardize our prospects of entering heaven, which is the supreme objective of both our lives. And I pray that God Himself will make our affection for one another perfect and eternal.

Isn't that a beautiful way to say "I love you"? How badly America needs husbands and fathers who are committed to their families— men who are *determined* to succeed in this important responsibility. My father was such a man, and his devotion to my mother grew steadily through their forty-three years of marriage. They were *mutually dependent* in the way God intended. It is fitting, therefore, that in his final moment of consciousness, he fell toward my mother and died peacefully in her arms.

Very few people fully comprehended the depth of my dad's love of learning. When he died, he left a book beside his big chair, opened to a description of the molecular structure of deoxyribonucleic acid and the process by which hereditary characteristics are transmitted from one generation to the next. Beside it was a list (in his handwriting) of the twenty essential amino acids in humans, and how they are genetically coded. (He called them "God's four-letter words"). My dad had an insatiable desire *to know*, alternating regularly between biology, physics, astronomy, ecology, theology, politics, medicine and the arts. He left a half-finished painting of a mountain stream in his basement, with a photograph propped to its right. A palette of oils still rests where he placed them on that final Saturday night. Yes, my dad loved *everything* God made, and it is thrilling to contemplate the learning process that must be occurring right now on the other side!

Finally, my dad also loved me. I've known that from my earliest moments of awareness. I'm told that when I was a small child, perhaps three years of age, we lived in a one-bedroom apartment. My little bed was located beside the bed of my parents. Dad said it was not uncommon during that time for him to awaken at night and hear a little voice whispering, "Daddy? Daddy?"

He would answer quietly, "What, Jimmy?"

Then I would reply, "Hold my hand!"

My dad would reach across the darkness and grope for my little hand, finally engulfing it in his. He said the instant he encompassed my hand, my arm would become limp and my breathing deep and regular. I had gone back to sleep. You see, I only wanted to know that he was *there!* I have been reaching for him throughout my forty-one years, and he has always been there. And now for the first time in my life, he's gone. ·

So where do we go from here? Do we leave this church today in despair and discouragement? Certainly not, although our sorrow is incalculable. But my dad is not in that casket before us. He is *alive,* and we will soon see him again. He has achieved the pearl of eternal life, which is our heritage, too. I now understand that the death of my dad was not an isolated tragedy that happened to one unfortunate man and his family. In a real sense, this is the human condition which affects us all. Life will soon be over for everyone in this sanctuary . . . and for everyone whom we love. · Therefore, I have determined to live each day as Christ would dictate, keeping in mind the temporal nature of everything which now seems so permanent. Even in death, you see, my dad has taught me about life.

Thank you for allowing me to share my deepest feelings and emotions, today. I must acknowledge, in closing, that James

---

·Seven members of our family have died in the past eighteen months: my father, Shirley's grandmother (Mrs. Hassie Wisham), my uncle (Dr. James McGraw), my aunt (Mrs. Naomi Dobson), my great uncle and aunt (Rev. and Mrs. R. M. Parks) and Shirley's uncle (Mr. Al Frasher).

Dobson was not a perfect man. It would be unfortunate to eulogize him in a way that would embarrass him if he were sitting among us. My father had a generous assortment of flaws, even as you and I. But I loved him. Perhaps . . . as much as any son ever loved his dad.

Danae and Ryan [addressed to my children], you had a great man for a grandfather. Not because he was President or because he will be remembered in the history books. He was great because of his uncompromising dedication to the Christian faith. And if I can be half the father to you that he was to me, you will be fortunate children, indeed.

"A sudden death is God's kiss upon the soul!"

—Anonymous

Chapter 2

The Revelation

Two years before my father's death, he shared an experience that occurred while he had been praying and reading the Bible. He seemed almost embarrassed to reveal the details, but I coaxed him to tell me the story. It involved an overwhelming impression, almost a divine decree, that he and I were going to cooperate on a very important project. He hastened to say that he didn't want me to think he was trying to "ride on my coattail." In fact, his first impulse was to tell no one about the revelation for fear that his motives would be misunderstood.

His apprehension was unfounded. I learned very early in life that when God "speaks" to Dad, I had better pay attention. This man and his Lord had a very unusual relationship. It often involved sessions of prayer and communion, lasting from four to

six hours, focusing especially on his ministry and on those whom
he loved. And when God revealed His purpose to His faithful
servant, the outcome was an absolute certainty.

But what task would we accomplish together? Neither of us
knew the answer to that question, nor did we pursue it further.
We did join forces to work on a conference book entitled *Family
under Fire*, but that didn't seem to be related to the revelation.
The months rolled by and the matter was filed under the broad
heading "Things I don't understand about the Lord."

Then came my father's initial heart attack while I was in San
Antonio. That devastating telephone conversation reverberated
in my head. "Your dad is dying. He has developed both
arhythmia and congestion, which is usually a fatal combination
following a myocardial infarction. We don't expect him to live
through the night. Come as quickly as you can get here!"

Two friends rushed me to the airport, where Shirley was
already waiting. But as we drove through the San Antonio
traffic, the Lord spoke to me. His voice was not audible, nor was
it accompanied by smoke and fire. I can't even tell you how the
message was conveyed. All I know is that God reminded me of
His revelation to my dad, and then said, "You are going to write
a book for husbands and fathers, based on the life of your dad.
The inspiration will be derived from his values, his dedication,
his walk with Me. This is the joint venture of which I spoke two
years ago."

As we made that long plane ride from San Antonio to Kansas
City, Shirley and I knew that my dad's condition would be
obvious instantly as we stepped into the terminal. If my mother
was there to meet us, that would mean he was gone. But if she
were not present, then she would still be with him at the
hospital. Upon disembarking from the plane, we scanned the
crowd breathlessly and to our great relief, Mother was not there.
Instead, we were greeted by the wife of the president of the
college where my father served as a professor. And she was
smiling.

"Your dad is remarkably better," she said. "In fact, he's waiting to see you at the hospital."

I will always be thankful for having the priceless opportunity to see him alive, again—to express those words of appreciation and love that we seldom convey before it is too late. I stood by his bed in that intensive care unit. There amidst beeping oscilloscopes and bottles of glucose, I patted those delicate artistic hands that I have loved since my earliest awareness. He was entirely calm and coherent, revealing no hint of his brush with death.

Then I told him about the Lord's message to me on the way to the airport. I explained that his part of the project was already completed: it involved sixty-six years of integrity and devotion and love. I had watched him at home throughout my childhood, where it was impossible to hide his true nature. But never one time did I see him compromise with evil or abandon the faith by which he had lived. His character had been like a beacon for me, illuminating my way and steering me past the snares that entrapped so many of my friends.

"Thank you, Dad," I said, with deep emotion.

He smiled knowingly, and I quietly slipped out of his room. Though the months have passed and he is now gone, that conversation lingers as I begin my part of the joint venture. Today, May 24, would have been his sixty-eighth birthday, and it is fitting that I use this occasion to describe the values for which he stood.

But this book is not intended as a biography of my dad's life, by any means. In fact, its primary theme actually originated three years before his death. I had asked the Lord, as a special favor, to reveal His message to the Christian family.

I prayed, "As long as I'm going to be speaking and writing and attempting to influence husbands and wives and children; I would like to know what *you* want me to convey. Why should I depend on my own puny insight and wisdom, when I can tap the resources of the Creator of families? Give me, then, the concepts that you want me to communicate."

Again, I experienced one of those quiet moments of awareness when I knew the Lord had spoken. It should be emphasized that for me, at least, these examples of unmistakable leadership from God are relatively infrequent events. More typically, I learn of His will through providential circumstances, doors that open or close, and so on. But on a few occasions, His desires have been communicated directly from His heart to mine.

Such was the case in response to my prayer for wisdom and insight (although it sounds terribly pompous and self-important to relate now). But this was God's reply, translated into my own words: "If America is going to survive the incredible stresses and dangers it now faces, it will be because husbands and fathers again place their families at the highest level on their system of priorities, reserving a portion of their time and energy for leadership within their homes!"

I have been dutifully conveying that message at every opportunity for the past five years. I've said it on the radio, on television, on audio cassettes and on film. The time has come, at last, to put it in writing, where the concept can be explored in its many dimensions. That brings us to this day.

Having described the background for this book, let me be honest about what it means to me. I suspect that authors often write a new manuscript in the same spirit that General Motors brings out a new model. It merely takes its place in a long line of creations, having no more significance than the one before or after. However, I feel that my message to men is the most critical topic I have ever addressed, and as such, may be the task for which I was born. The Western world stands at a great crossroads in its history. And it is my opinion, based on the experience I shared, that our very survival as a people will depend on the presence or absence of masculine leadership in millions of homes.

Why do I place such importance on the involvement of *men* in determining the survival of a culture? Because no modern society can exceed the stability of its individual family units, and women seem more aware of that fact than their husbands. Consider the evidence. Who reads the books on family living? Eighty percent are known to be women. Who attends seminars on meaningful family life? The majority are women. Who enrolls in Bible study classes devoted to Scriptural underpinnings of the family? Women outnumber men by an incredible margin. Who listens to family radio programs and cassette tapes on marriage and parenthood? Once again, they are likely to be female.

What I'm saying is that Christian women, to a large extent, are already motivated to preserve their families. And though I hate to admit it, women often know more than their husbands about the role God has ordained for men. One of the most common letters I receive is sent by hundreds of women who ask the same question:

> My husband won't assume spiritual leadership in our family. He doesn't seem to be aware of my needs and the requirements of our children. How can I get his attention?

That's why I believe, with everything within me, that husbands hold the *keys* to the preservation of the family. If we can get men to slow down long enough to look at the issues, some will make the changes necessary for survival. And I'm certain that their wives will follow suit.

Derek Prince expressed his view that the major problems facing the Western world can be traced to what he called "renegade males." A renegade is defined as "one who reneges." It is a harsh indictment, but there is validity in the assessment. God has charged men with the responsibility for providing leadership in their homes and families: leadership in the form of loving authority; leadership in the form of financial management; leadership in the form of spiritual training; and leadership in maintaining the marital relationship. Husbands are instructed to "love [their] wives, just as Christ loved the Church and gave himself up for her" (Eph. 5:25, NIV). That is not a casual suggestion to Christian men; it is God's *commandment* to husbands and fathers.

The purpose of this book, then, is to sound a call to arms. But more than that, I hope to offer a redefinition of masculinity. The Judeo-Christian concept of manliness has been blurred by the Women's Liberation Movement, which has not only brought into question everything traditionally feminine, but has confused men as well. The "macho man" is portrayed by the media as an anachronism. The sit-com father on television is invariably a bumbling fool who has trouble remembering his name and address. This concerted attack on "maleness" has damaged or destroyed the notion of what a good father is . . . what a loving husband does.

My father exemplified what I believe to be God's concept of masculinity. Perhaps, through him, we can reconstruct a model that will bear the approval of the Creator Himself.

Chapter 3

What Is a Man?

DURING THE CHRISTMAS season 1969, my father's two surviving brothers and his sister gathered in California for a family reunion. And on that happy occasion, they spent the better part of five days reminiscing about their childhood and early home life. One of the grandchildren had enough initiative to record the discussions on cassette tapes, and I was privileged to obtain a complete set. What a rich heritage this provided, granting insight into my grandparents' home and the early experiences of my dad.

While all the conversations were of interest to me, there was a common thread that was especially significant throughout the week. It focused on the *respect* with which these four siblings addressed the memory of their father (my grandfather). He died in 1935, a year before my birth, yet they spoke of him with an unmistakable awe more than thirty-four years later. He still lived in their minds as a man of enormous character and strength.

I asked them to explain the qualities that they admired so greatly, but received little more than vague generalities.

"He was a tower of strength," said one.

"He had a certain dignity about him," said another, with appropriate gestures.

"We held him in awe," replied the third.

It is difficult to summarize the subtleties and complexities of the human personality, and they were unable to find the right words. Only when we began talking about specific remembrances did the personality of this patriarch become apparent. My dad provided the best evidence by writing his recollection of Grandfather Dobson's death, which I've reproduced below. Flowing throughout this narrative is the impact of a great man on his family, even three decades after his demise.

The Last Days of R. L. Dobson

The attack that took his life occurred when he was sixty-nine years of age, and resulted ultimately in the breakup of the family circle. For many years after his death, I could not pass Tri-State Hospital without noting one particular window. It stood out from the rest, hallowed because it represented the room where he had suffered so much. The details of those tragic days and nights remain in my memory, unchanged by the passage of time.

We had been three days and three nights practically without sleep, listening to him struggle for breath, hearing the sounds of approaching death, smelling the smells of death. Dad lay in a deep coma. His heavy breathing could be heard up and down the corridor. We walked the halls of that old hospital for hours listening to the ceaseless struggle which now was becoming fainter and fainter. Several times the nurse had called us in and we had said the last "goodbye"—had gone through the agony of giving him up, only to have his heart rally, and then the endless vigil would begin all over again. Finally, we had gone into an adjoining room not prepared for sleep, but some in the chairs and some across the beds, we had fallen into the sleep of utter exhaustion.

At five minutes to four o'clock the nurse came in and awakened one of my twin brothers. Robert roused with a start. "Is he gone?" he asked.

"No, but if you boys want to see your dad one more time while he is alive, you'd better come, now."

The word quickly passed around and we filed into the room to stand around his bed for the last time. I remember that I stood at his left side: I smoothed back the hair from his forehead, and laid my hand on his big old red hand, so very much like my own. I felt the fever that precedes death: 105. While I was standing there a change came over me. Instead of being a grown man (I was twenty-four at the time) I became a little boy again. They say this often happens to adults who witness the death of a parent. I thought I was in the Union Train Station in Shreveport, Louisiana, in the late afternoon, and I was watching for his return. The old Kansas City Southern passenger train was backing into the station and I saw it come 'round the curve. My heart swelled with pride. I turned to the little boy standing next to me and said, "You see that big man standing on the back of the train, one hand on the air brake and the other on the little whistle with which he signals the engineer? That big man is my dad!" He set the air brakes and I heard the wheels grind to a stop. I saw him step off that last coach. I ran and jumped into his arms. I gave him a tight hug and I smelled the train smoke on his clothes. "Daddy, I love you," I said.

It all comes back. I patted that big hand and said "Goodbye, Dad," as he was sinking fast, now. "We haven't forgotten how hard you worked to send five boys and one girl through college: how you wore those old conductor uniforms until they were slick—doing without—that we might have things that we didn't really need. . . ."

At three minutes to four o'clock, like a stately ship moving slowly out of time's harbor into eternity's sea, he breathed his last. The nurse motioned us to leave, and pulled the sheet over his head, a gesture that struck terror to my heart, and we turned with silent

26

weeping to leave the room. Then an incident occurred that I will never forget. Just as we got to the door, I put my arm around my little mother and said, "Mama, this is awful."

Dabbing at her eyes with her handkerchief, she said, "Yes, Jimmy, but there is one thing Mother wants you to remember, now. We have said 'good night' down here, but one of these days we are going to say 'good morning' up there."

I believe she did say "good morning" too, eleven years later, and I know he met her "just inside the Eastern gate."

His death was marked by quietness and dignity, just like the life he had lived. Thus came to an end the affairs of R. L. Dobson, and thus ended, too, the solidarity of the family. The old home place was never to be the same again. The old spirit that we had known as children was gone forever!

Though this illustration reveals few of the specific characteristics that made R. L. Dobson such a powerful influence in his family, it does tell us how his son felt about him. I happen to know some of the other details. He was a man of absolute integrity and honesty. Though not a Christian until shortly before his death, he lived by an internal standard that was singularly uncompromising. As a young man, for example, he invested heavily in a business venture with a partner whom he later discovered to be dishonest. When he learned of the chicanery, he virtually gave the company to the other man. That former partner built the corporation into one of the most successful operations in the South, and became a multimillionaire. But my grandfather never looked back. He took a clean conscience with him to his grave.

There were other admirable traits, of course, and many of them were transmitted to my dad. These two men personified much of what I'm trying to convey in this examination of masculinity. My father added the dimension of *vulnerability* to the pattern, which is beautifully captured in the drawing by Ray Craighead (his art student) reproduced on the final page of this book.

Having looked superficially at the image of two strong fathers and their influence at home, let's turn now to the specifics. We'll discuss the interaction of a man with his children, his wife, his work, and his God, among related subjects. And as we do, may I make a suggestion for those who enjoy a personal relationship with the Lord? You might pause to ask Him, *prior* to reading those chapters, what new understandings He wishes to convey through the pages of this book. It is my desire that He speak to each family (and especially to each man) in the terms we need to hear.

A MAN AND HIS CHILDREN

Chapter 4

A Man and His Children

I WAS WALKING toward my car outside a shopping center a few weeks ago, when I heard a loud and impassioned howl.

"Auggghh!" groaned the masculine voice.

I spotted a man about fifty feet away who was in great distress (and for a very good reason). His fingers were caught in the jamb of a car door which had obviously been slammed unexpectedly. Then the rest of the story unfolded. Crouching in the front seat was an impish little three-year-old boy who had apparently decided to "close the door on Dad."

The father was pointing frantically at his fingers with his free hand, and saying, "Oh! Oh! Open the door, Chuckie! They're caught . . . hurry . . . Chuckie . . . please . . . open . . . OPEN!"

Chuckie finally got the message and unlocked the door, releasing Dad's blue fingers. The father then hopped and jumped around the aisles of the parking lot, alternately kissing and caressing his battered hand. Chuckie sat unmoved in the front seat of their car, waiting for Pop to settle down.

I know this incident was painful to the man who experienced it, but I must admit that it struck me funny. I suppose his plight symbolized the enormous cost of parenthood. And yes, Virginia, it *is* expensive to raise boys and girls today. Parents give the best they have to their children, who often respond by slamming the door on their "fingers"—especially during the unappreciative adolescent years. Perhaps that is why someone quipped, "Insanity is an inherited disease. You get it from your kids."

But there are other things that we get from our kids, including love and meaning and purpose and an opportunity to give. They also help us maintain our sense of humor, which is essential to emotional stability in these stressful days. I'm reminded of Anne Ortlund's eleven-year-old son whom she described in her book *Disciplines of a Beautiful Woman.* She had taken this rambunctious boy to their pediatrician for a routine physical examination. Before seeing the doctor, however, the nurse weighed and measured the child and attempted to obtain a medical history.

"Tell me, Mrs. Ortlund," said the nurse, "how is he sleeping?"

Nels answered on his own behalf, "I sleep very well." The nurse wrote that down.

"How's his appetite, Mrs. Ortlund?"

"I eat everything," said Nels. She wrote that down.

"Mrs. Ortlund, how are his bowels?"

The boy responded, "A, E, I, O and U." *

Those memories are priceless to the parent who isn't too tired

---

* Waco, Texas: Word Books, 1977, p. 92.

to notice. Let me share one more true story. A father told me recently about a five-year-old boy who was sitting on the toilet at the precise instant an earthquake rocked Los Angeles County on February 9, 1971. The jolt was so severe that it knocked this lad off the potty. But never having been in an earthquake before, he thought the rumble had been caused by his *own* bathroom activity. "What did I do, Mom?" he asked, with childlike wonder.

A family is literally a "museum of memories" to those who have been blessed by the presence of children. Although my kids are now fourteen and nine, I can recall ten thousand episodes that are carefully preserved in my mind. The "videotapes" of their early years are among my most valued possessions: even now, I see a six-year-old girl coming home from school. Her hair is disheveled and one sock is down around her ankle. It is obvious that she's been spinning upside down on the playground bars. She asks for a glass of milk and sits down at the kitchen table, unaware of the tenderness and love that I feel for her at that moment. Then she runs out to play.

Another "tape" begins to roll. I see a four-year-old boy with a Band-aid on his knee and bread crumbs on his face. He approaches my chair and asks to sit on my lap.

"Sorry," I said. "Only one boy in the world can climb on me when he chooses."

"Whoizzat?" he replies.

"Oh, you wouldn't know him. He's a kid named Ryan."

"But my name is Ryan!"

"Yes, but the boy I'm talking about has blond hair and blue eyes."

"Don't you see my blond hair? And my eyes are blue."

"Yes, but many kids have those. The only boy who can get on my lap is my son . . . my only son . . . whom I love."

"Hey, that's me! I'm your son. My name is Ryan! And I'm coming up!"

That little game has been played for seven years, and it still has meaning.

But I can hear my readers saying, "You're just a sentimentalist."

"You bet I am!" I reply. I'm not ashamed to admit that *people* matter to me, and I'm most vulnerable to those people within my own family. I've enjoyed every stage in the lives of our two kids and wish that they (we) could remain young forever.

Not only have Shirley and I enjoyed the developmental years, but Danae and Ryan have apparently shared that appreciation. Our daughter, especially, has loved every aspect of childhood and has been most reluctant to leave it. Her phonograph records and her stuffed animals and her bedroom have been prized possessions since toddlerhood. Likewise, she sat on Santa's lap for four years after she knew he was a phony. But, alas, she turned thirteen years old and began hearing a new set of drums. About a year ago, she went through her toys and records, stacking them neatly and leaving them in front of Ryan's bedroom door. On the top was a note which Shirley brought to me with tears in her eyes. It read:

> Dear Ryan:
>
> These are yours now.
> Take good care of them
> like I have.
> Love,
> Danae

That brief message signaled the closing of the door called "Childhood." And once it shut, no power on earth could open it again. That's why the toddler and elementary school years should be seen as fleeting opportunities. Yet this priceless period of influence often occurs at a time when fathers are the least accessible to their kids. They are trying to establish themselves in their occupations, racing and running and huffing and puffing, dragging home a briefcase crammed to the brim with night work, scurrying to the airport to catch the last plane to Chicago, moonlighting to pay those vacation bills, and finally collapsing in bed in a state of utter exhaustion. Another day has passed with no interchange between Dad and his teachable little boy or girl.

One mother told me of hearing her preschool son talking to another four-year-old boy on the front steps.

"Where is your daddy?" he asked. "I've never seen him."

"Oh, he doesn't *live* here," came the reply. "He only *sleeps* here."

Without wanting to heap guilt on the heads of my masculine readers, I must say that too many fathers only *sleep* at their homes. And as a result, they have totally abdicated their responsibilities for leadership and influence in the lives of their children. I cited a study in my previous book *What Wives Wish Their Husbands Knew About Women* that documented the problem of inaccessible fathers. Let me quote from that source.

The August 1974 issue of *Scientific American* included an important article entitled "The Origins of Alienation," by Urie Bronfenbrenner. Dr. Bronfenbrenner is, in my opinion, the foremost authority on child development in America today, and his views should be considered carefully. In this article, Dr. Bronfenbrenner discussed the deteriorating status of the American family and the forces which are weakening its cohesiveness. More specifically, he is concerned about the circumstances which are seriously undermining parental love and depriving children of the leadership and love they must have for survival.

One of those circumstances is widely known as the "rat-race." Dr. Bronfenbrenner described the problem this way, "The demands of a job that claim mealtimes, evenings and weekends as well as days; the trips and moves necessary to get ahead or simply to hold one's own; the increasing time spent commuting, entertaining, going out, meeting social and community obligations . . . all of these produce a situation in which a child often spends more time with a passive babysitter than with a participating parent."

According to Dr. Bronfenbrenner, this rat race is particularly incompatible with fatherly responsibilities, as illustrated by a recent investigation which yielded startling results. A team of researchers wanted to learn how much time middle-class fathers spend playing and interacting with their small children. First, they asked a group of fathers to estimate the time spent with their one-year-old youngsters each day, and received an average reply of fifteen to twenty minutes. To verify these claims, the investigators attached microphones to the shirts of small children for the purpose of recording actual parental verbalization. The results of this study are shocking: The average amount of time spent by these middle-class fathers with their small children was thirty-seven seconds per day! Their direct interaction was limited to 2.7 encounters daily, lasting ten to fifteen seconds each! That, so it seems, represents the contribution of fatherhood for millions of America's children.*

Let's compare the thirty-seven-second interchanges between fathers and small children with another statistic. The average preschool child watches between 30 and 50 hours of television per week (the figures vary from one study to another). What an incredible picture is painted by those two statistics. During the formative years of life, when children are so vulnerable to their experiences, they're receiving thirty-seven seconds a day from their fathers and thirty or more hours a week from commercial television! Need we ask where our kids are getting their values?

Someone observed, "Values are not *taught* to our children; they are *caught* by them." It is true. Seldom can we get little Johnny or Mary to sit patiently on a chair while we lecture to them about God and the other important issues of life. Instead, they are equipped with internal "motors" which are incapable of idling. Their transmissions consist of only six gears: run, jump,

---

*James C. Dobson, *What Wives Wish Their Husbands Knew About Women* (Wheaton, IL: Tyndale House, 1975), pp. 157–58.

climb, crawl, slide and dive. Boys and girls are simply not wired for quiet conversations about heavy topics.

How, then, do conscientious parents convey their attitudes and values and faith to their children? It is done *subtly*, through the routine interactions of everyday living.* We saw this fact illustrated in our own home when Danae was ten years old and Ryan was five. We were riding in the car when we passed a porno theater. I believe the name of the particular movie was "Flesh Gordon," or something equally sensuous. Danae, who was sitting in the front seat, pointed to the theater and said,

"That's a dirty movie, isn't it, Dad?"

I nodded affirmatively.

"Is that what they call an X-rated movie?" she asked.

Again, I indicated that she was correct.

Danae thought for a moment or two, then said, "Dirty movies are really bad, aren't they?"

I said, "Yes, Danae. Dirty movies are very evil."

This entire conversation lasted less than a minute, consisting of three brief questions and three replies. Ryan, who was in the back seat, did not enter into our discussion. In fact, I wondered what he thought about the interchange, and concluded that he probably wasn't listening.

I was wrong. Ryan heard the conversation and apparently continued thinking about it for several days. But amusingly, Ryan did not know what a "dirty movie" was. How would a five-year-old boy learn what goes on in such places, since no one had ever discussed pornography with him? Nevertheless, he had his own idea about the subject. That concept was revealed to me four nights later at the close of the day.

Ryan and I got down on our knees to say his bedtime prayer, and the preschooler spontaneously returned to that conversation earlier in the week.

---

* See Deut. 6:4–9.

"Dear Lord," he began in great seriousness, "help me not to go see any dirty movies . . . where everyone is spitting on each other."

For Ryan, the dirtiest thing he could imagine would be a salivary free-for-all. That *would* be dirty, I had to admit.

But I also had to acknowledge how *casually* children assimilate our values and attitudes. You see, I had no way of anticipating that brief conversation in the car. It was not my deliberate intention to convey my views about pornography to my children. How was it that they learned one more dimension of my value system on that morning? It occurred because we happened to be together . . . to be talking to one another. Those kinds of subtle, unplanned interactions account for much of the instruction that passes from one generation to the next. It is a powerful force in shaping young lives, *if!* If parents are occasionally at home with their kids; *if* they have the energy to converse with them; *if* they have anything worthwhile to transmit; *if* they care.

My point is that the breathless American lifestyle is particularly costly to children. Yet 1.8 million youngsters come home to an empty house after school each day. They are called "latchkey" kids because they wear the keys to their front doors around their necks. Not only are their fathers overcommitted and preoccupied, but now, their mothers are energetically seeking fulfillment in the working world, too. So who is at home with the kids? More commonly, the answer is *nobody*.

A popular song beautifully portrays the cost of overcommitment in family life. It was written by Sandy and Harry Chapin, who titled it "Cat's in the Cradle." I've obtained permission to reproduce the lyrics, as follows, specifically for the fathers who are reading this book:

A Man and His Children

CAT'S IN THE CRADLE

By Sandy and Harry Chapin

My child arrived just the other day
  he came to the world in the usual way—
  But there were planes to catch and bills to pay
  he learned to walk while I was away
    and he was talkin fore I knew it and as he grew
          he'd say

    I'm gonna be like you, Dad
    you know I'm gonna be like you.

  and the cat's in the cradle and the silver spoon
  Little boy blue and the man in the moon
  when you comin' home, Dad
      I don't know when
      but we'll get together then—
    you know we'll have a good time then

My son turned 10 just the other day
  he said, Thanks for the ball, Dad, com'on let's play
  Can you teach me to throw?
  I said not today, I got a lot to do
  He said, That's okay
    and he walked away but his smile never dimmed
  it said I'm gonna be like him, yeah
    you know I'm gonna be like him

  and the cat's in the cradle and the silver spoon
  Little boy blue and the man in the moon
  when you comin' home, Dad

> I don't know when
> but we'll get together then—
> you know we'll have a good time then

Well he came home from college just the other day
so much like a man I just had to say
Son, I'm proud of you, can you sit for awhile
He shook his head and said with a smile—
what I'd really like, Dad, is to borrow the car keys
see you later, can I have them please?

When you comin home, Son?
> I don't know when
> but we'll get together then
> you know we'll have a good time then

I've long since retired, my son's moved away
I called him up just the other day
I said I'd like to see you if you don't mind
He said, I'd love to, Dad—if I can find the time

You see my new job's a hassle and the kids have the flu
but it's sure nice talkin to you, Dad
It's been nice talking to you

And as I hung up the phone, it occurred to me—
he'd grown up just like me; my boy was just like me

and the cat's in the cradle and the silver spoon
Little boy blue and the man in the moon
when you comin home, Son?
> I don't know when
> but we'll get together then, Dad,
> we're gonna have a good time then

Do those words strike home to anyone but me? Have *you* felt
the years slipping by with far too many unfulfilled promises to
your children? Have you heard yourself saying,

40

"Son, we've been talking about that wagon we were going to build one of these Saturdays, and I just want you to know that I haven't forgotten it. But we can't do it this weekend 'cause I have to make an unexpected trip to Indianapolis. However, we *will* get to it one of these days. I'm not sure if it can be next weekend, but you keep reminding me and we'll eventually work together. And I'm going to take you fishing, too. I *love* to fish and I know a little stream that is jumping with trout in the Spring. But this just happens to be a very busy month for your mom and me, so let's keep planning and before you know it, the time will be here."

Then the days soon become weeks, and the weeks flow into months and years and decades . . . and our kids grow up and leave home. Then we sit in the silence of our family rooms, trying to recall the precious experiences that escaped us there. Ringing in our ears is that haunting phrase, "We'll have a good time . . . then . . ."

Oh, I know I'm stirring a measure of guilt into the pot with these words. But perhaps we need to be confronted with the important issues of life, even if they make us uncomfortable. Furthermore, I feel *obligated* to speak on behalf of the millions of children across this country who are reaching for fathers who aren't there. The names of specific boys and girls come to my mind as I write these words, symbolizing the masses of lonely kids who experience the agony of unmet needs. Let me acquaint you with two or three of those children whose paths I have crossed.

I think, first, of the mother who approached me after I had spoken a few years ago. She had supported her husband through college and medical school, only to have him divorce her in favor of a younger plaything. She stood with tears in her eyes as she described the impact of his departure on her two sons.

"They miss their daddy every day," she said. "They don't understand why he doesn't come to see them. The older boy, especially, wants a father so badly that he reaches for every man who comes into our lives. What can I tell him? How can I meet the boy's needs for a father who will hunt and fish and play football and bowl with him and his brother? It's breaking my heart to see them suffer so much."

I gave this mother a few suggestions and offered my understanding and support. The next morning I spoke for the final time at her church. Following the service, I stood on the platform as a line of people waited to tell me goodbye and extend their greetings. Standing in the line was the mother *with* her two sons.

They greeted me with smiles and I shook the older child's hand. Then something happened which I did not recall until I was on my way back to Los Angeles. The boy did not let go of my hand! He gripped it tightly, preventing me from welcoming others who pressed around. To my regret, I realized later that I had unconsciously grasped his arm with my other hand, pulling myself free from his grip. I sat on the plane, realizing the full implications of that incident. You see, this lad *needed* me. He needed a man who could take the place of his renegade father. And I had failed him, just like all the rest. Now I'm left with the memory of a child who said with his eyes, "Could you be a daddy to me?"!

Another child has found a permanent place in my memory, although I don't even know her name. I was waiting to catch a plane at Los Angeles International Airport, enjoying my favorite activity of "people watching." But I was unprepared for the drama about to unfold. Standing near me was an old man who obviously waited for someone who should have been on the plane that arrived minutes before. He examined each face intently as the passengers filed past. I thought he seemed unusually distressed as he waited.

Then I saw the little girl who stood by his side. She must have been seven years old, and she, too, was desperately looking for a certain face in the crowd. I have rarely seen a child more anxious than this cute little girl. She clung to the old man's arm, whom I assumed to be her grandfather. Then as the last passengers came by, one by one, the girl began to cry silently. She was not merely disappointed in that moment; her little heart was broken. The grandfather also appeared to be fighting back the tears. In fact, he was too upset to comfort the child, who then buried her face in the sleeve of his worn coat.

"Oh, God!" I prayed silently. "What special agony are they experiencing in this hour? Was it the child's mother who abandoned her on that painful day? Did her daddy promise to come and then change his mind?"

My great impulse was to throw my arms around the little girl and shield her from the awfulness of that hour. I wanted her to pour out her grief in the protection of my embrace, but I feared that my intrusion would be misunderstood. So I watched helplessly. Then the old man and the child stood silently as the passengers departed from two other planes, but the anxiety on their faces had turned to despair. Finally, they walked slowly through the terminal and toward the door. Their only sound was the snuffing of the little girl who fought to control her tears.

Where is this child now? God only knows.

If the reader will bear with me, I must introduce you to one other child whose family experience has become so common in the Western world. I was waiting at Shawnee Mission Hospital for word on my dad's heart condition, after he was stricken in September. There in the waiting room was an *American Girl* magazine which caught my attention. (I must have been desperate for something to read to have been attracted to the *American Girl*.)

I opened the cover page and immediately saw a composition written by a fourteen-year-old girl named Vicki Kraushaar. She had submitted her story for publication in the section of the magazine entitled "By You." I'll let Vicki introduce herself and describe her experience.

That's the Way Life Goes Sometimes

When I was ten, my parents got a divorce. Naturally, my father told me about it, because he was my favorite. [Notice that Vicki did not say, *"I was his favorite."*]

"Honey, I know it's been kind of bad for you these past few days, and I don't want to make it worse. But there's something I have to tell you. Honey, your mother and I got a divorce."

"But, Daddy—"

"I know you don't want this, but it has to be done. Your mother and I just don't get along like we used to. I'm already packed and my plane is leaving in half an hour."

"But, Daddy, why do you have to leave?"

"Well, honey, your mother and I can't live together anymore."

"I know that, but I mean why do you have to leave town?"

"Oh. Well, I got someone waiting for me in New Jersey."

"But, Daddy, will I ever see you again?"

"Sure you will, honey. We'll work something out."

"But what? I mean, you'll be living in New Jersey, and I'll be living here in Washington."

"Maybe your mother will agree to you spending two weeks in the summer and two in the winter with me."

"Why not more often?"

"I don't think she'll agree to two weeks in the summer and two in the winter, much less more."

"Well, it can't hurt to try."

"I know, honey, but we'll have to work it out later. My plane leaves in twenty minutes and I've got to get to the airport. Now I'm going to get my luggage, and I want you to go to your room so you don't have to watch me. And no long goodbyes either."

"Okay, Daddy. Goodbye. Don't forget to write."

"I won't. Goodbye. Now go to your room."

"Okay. Daddy, I don't want you to go!"

"I know, honey. But I have to."

"Why?"

"You wouldn't understand, honey."

"Yes, I would."

"No, you wouldn't."

"Oh well. Goodbye."

"Goodbye. Now go to your room. Hurry up."

"Okay. Well, I guess that's the way life goes sometimes."

"Yes honey. That's the way life goes sometimes."

After my father walked out that door, I never heard from him again. *

Vicki speaks eloquently on behalf of a million American children who have heard those shattering words, "Honey, your mother and I are getting a divorce." Across this country, husbands and wives are responding to the media blitz which urges and goads them to do their own thing, to chase impulsive desires without regard for the welfare of their families.

"The kids will get over it," goes the rationalization.

Every form of mass communication seems mobilized to spread the "me first" philosophy. Frank Sinatra said it musically in his song *"I did it my way."* Sammy Davis, Jr., echoed the sentiment in "I've gotta be me." Robert J. Ringer provided the literary version in *Looking Out for Number One*, which became the best-selling book in America for forty-six weeks. It was flanked by *Open Marriage, Creative Divorce*, and *Pulling Your Own Strings*, among hundreds of other dangerous best sellers. The est program now sells the same sickness under the guise of psychological health.

It all sounds so noble in theory. It's called "the discovery of personhood," and it offers an intoxicating appeal to our selfish lusts. But when this insidious philosophy has wormed its way into our system of values, it begins to rot us from within. First, it encourages an insignificant flirtation with sin (perhaps with a man or woman from New Jersey) followed by passion and illicit sexual encounters, followed by camouflaging lies and deceit, followed by angry words and sleepless nights, followed by tears

---

*Reprinted by permission from *American Girl*, a magazine for all girls published by Girl Scouts of the U.S.A.

and anguish, followed by crumbling self-esteem, followed by attorneys and divorce courts and property settlements, followed by devastating custody hearings. And from deep within the maelstrom, we can hear the cry of three wounded children—two girls and a boy—who will never fully recover. "Then when lust hath conceived, it bringeth forth sin; and sin, when it is finished, bringeth forth death" (James 1:15, KJV).

Lest I sound self-righteous and "preachy," let me focus the glaring spotlight on my own inadequacies. While I have never been involved in an affair, *nor will I ever,* there have certainly been times when I have permitted overcommitment to rob my children of my involvement. I'll reveal the details in the following chapter for those who have the inclination to continue.

My father often quoted Eugene Field's Little Boy Blue" to me when I was a child. This poem has always been a favorite, but it has assumed new meaning since the birth of my children.

Little Boy Blue

The little toy dog is covered with dust,
    But sturdy and staunch he stands;
And the little toy soldier is red with rust,
    And his musket moulds in his hands.
Time was when the little toy dog was new,
    And the soldier was passing fair;
And that was the time when our Little Boy Blue
    Kissed them and put them there.

A Man and His Children

"Now, don't you go till I come," he said,
  "And don't you make any noise!"
So, toddling off to his trundle-bed,
  He dreamt of the pretty toys;
And, as he was dreaming, an angel song
  Awakened our Little Boy Blue—
Oh! the years are many, the years are long,
  But the little toy friends are True!

Ay, faithful to Little Boy Blue they stand,
  Each in the same old place—
Awaiting the touch of a little hand,
  The smile of a little face;
And they wonder, as waiting the long years through
  In the dust of that little chair,
What has become of our Little Boy Blue
  Since he kissed them and put them there.

Eugene Field
1850–1895

Chapter 5

A Man and
His Ultimate Priority

IT OCCURRED FIRST in 1969, when *Dare to Discipline* was being written. I was running at an incredible speed, working myself to death like every other man I knew. I was Superintendent of Youth for my church, and labored under a heavy speaking schedule. Eight or ten "unofficial" responsibilities were added to my full-time commitment at USC School of Medicine and Children's Hospital of Los Angeles. I once worked seventeen nights straight without being home in the evening. Our five-year-old daughter would stand in the doorway and cry as I left in the morning, knowing she might not see me until the next sunrise.

Although my activities were bringing me professional advancement and the trappings of financial success, my dad was not impressed. He had observed my hectic lifestyle and felt obligated to express his concern. While flying from Los Angeles to Hawaii one summer, he used that quiet opportunity to write me a lengthy letter. It was to have a sweeping influence on my life. Let me quote one paragraph from his message which was especially poignant:

> Danae [referring to our daughter] is growing up in the wickedest section of a world much farther gone into moral decline than the world into which you were born. I have observed that the greatest delusion is to suppose that our children will be devout Christians simply because their parents have been, or that any of them will enter into the Christian faith in any other way than through their parents' deep travail of prayer and faith. But this prayer demands time, time that cannot be given if it is all signed and conscripted and laid on the altar of career ambition. Failure for you at this point would make mere success in your occupation a very pale and washed-out affair, indeed.

Those words, written without accusation or insult, hit me like the blow from a hammer. It contained several themes which had the ring of eternal truth. First, it *is* more difficult to teach proper values today than in years past because of the widespread rejection of Christian principles in our culture. In effect, there are many dissonant voices which feverishly contradict everything for which Christianity stands. The result is a generation of young people who have discarded the moral standards of the Bible. Consider the findings of U.C.L.A. sex researcher Aaron Hass as reported in his 1979 publication *Teenage Sexuality.* * Basing his investigation on questionnaires completed by 625 boys and girls in five states, he drew several striking conclusions. Among students between fifteen and sixteen years of age, forty-

---

* Macmillan, 1979.

three percent of the boys and thirty-one percent of the girls have had sexual intercourse. Twenty-eight percent of the boys and seven percent of the girls report having had at least *ten sexual partners*. Furthermore, among those seventeen to eighteen years old, more than nine-tenths of the boys and two-thirds of the girls approve of oral sex, and more than half of each group has experienced it! That is the world in which our children will be raised!

The second concept in my dad's letter was the one that ended my parental complacency. He helped me realize that it is possible for mothers and fathers to love and revere God while systematically losing their children. You can go to church three times a week, serve on its governing board, attend the annual picnic, pay your tithes and make all the approved religious noises, yet somehow fail to communicate the real meaning of Christianity to the next generation.

I have since talked to dozens of parents whose children are grown and married.

"We thought our kids had accepted our faith and beliefs," they say, "but somehow, we failed to get it across."

For those younger parents whose children are still at an impressionable age, please believe the words of my dad, "The greatest delusion is to suppose that our children will be devout Christians simply because their parents have been, or that *any* of them will enter into the Christian faith in any other way than through their parents deep travail of prayer and faith."

If you doubt the validity of this assertion, may I suggest that you read the story of Eli in 1 Samuel 2–4. Here is the account of a priest and servant of God who failed to discipline his children. He was apparently too busy with the "work of the church" to be a leader in his own home. The two boys grew up to be evil young men on whom God's judgment fell.

It concerned me to realize that Eli's service to the Lord was insufficient to compensate for his failures at home. Then I read farther in the narrative and received confirmation of the principle. *Samuel,* the saintly man of God who stood like a tower of spiritual strength throughout his life, grew up in Eli's home. He watched Eli systematically losing his children, yet Samuel proceeded to fail with his family, too! That was a deeply disturbing truth. If God would not honor Samuel's dedication by guaranteeing the salvation of his children, will He do more for *me* if I'm too busy to do my "homework"!

Having been confronted with these spiritual obligations and responsibilities, the Lord then gave me an enormous burden for my two children. I carry it to this day. There are times when it becomes so heavy that I ask God to remove it from my shoulders, although the concern is not motivated by the usual problems or anxieties. Our kids are apparently healthy and seem to be holding their own emotionally and academically. The source of my burden derives from the awareness that a "tug of war" is being waged for the hearts and minds of every child on earth, including these two precious human beings. Satan would deceive and destroy them if given the opportunity, and they will soon have to choose the path they will take.

This mission of introducing one's children to the Christian faith can be likened to a three-man relay race. First, your father runs his lap around the track, carrying the baton, which represents the gospel of Jesus Christ. At the appropriate moment, he hands the baton to you, and you begin your journey around the track. Then finally, the time will come when you must get the baton safely in the hands of your child. But as any track coach will testify, *relay races are won or lost in the transfer of the baton.* There is a critical moment when all can be lost by a fumble or miscalculation. The baton is rarely dropped on the back side of the track when the runner has it firmly in his grasp. If failure is to occur, it will likely happen in the exchange between generations!

According to the Christian values which govern my life, my most important reason for living is to get the baton—the gospel—safely in the hands of my children. Of course, I want to place it in as many other hands as possible, and I'm deeply devoted to the ministry to families that God has given me. *Nevertheless, my number one responsibility is to evangelize my own children.* In the words of my dad, everything else appears "pale and washed out" when compared with that fervent desire. Unless my son and daughter grasp the faith and take it with them around the track, it matters little how fast they run. Being first across the finish line is meaningless unless they carry the baton with them.

The urgency of this mission has taken Shirley and me to our knees since before the birth of our first child. Furthermore, since October 1971, I have designated one day a week for fasting and prayer specifically devoted to the spiritual welfare of our children. Shirley joined me in that venture for several years, until she became physically unable to participate every week. This commitment springs from an intense awareness of our need for divine assistance in the awesome task of parenthood. There is not enough knowledge in the books—not enough human wisdom anywhere on earth—to guarantee the outcome of parenting. There are too many factors beyond our control—too many evil influences—that mitigate against the Christian message. That is why we find ourselves in prayer, week after week, uttering this familiar petition:

Lord, here we are again. You know what we need even before we ask, but let us say it one more time. When you consider the many requests we have made of you through the years . . . regarding our health and my ministry and the welfare of our loved ones . . . please put this supplication at the *top* of the list: keep the circle of our little family unbroken when we stand before you on the Day of Judgment. Compensate for our mistakes and failures as parents, and counteract the influences of an evil world that would undermine the faith of our children. And especially, Lord, we ask for your involvement when our son and daughter stand at the crossroads, deciding whether or not to walk the Christian path. They will be beyond our care at that moment, and we humbly ask You to *be there.* Send a significant friend or leader to help them choose the right direction. They were yours before they were born, and now we give them back to you in faith, knowing that you love them even more than we do. Toward that end, we dedicate this day of fasting and prayer.

Not only has God heard this prayer, but He has blessed it in ways that we did not anticipate in the beginning. First, it has represented a project which Shirley and I have enjoyed *together*, drawing us closer to one another as we drew closer to God. Secondly, this act of fasting each week serves to remind us continually of our system of priorities. It is very difficult to forget your highest values when one day out of seven is spent concentrating on them. Finally, and most importantly, the children have seen this act of discipline every Tuesday, and have been influenced by it. Conversations similar to the one below occurred during the early 1970s:

"Why are you not eating dinner with us tonight, Dad?"

"This is Tuesday and I'm fasting today."

"Oh, yeah—what did you say 'fasting' meant?"

"Well, some Christians go without food during a short time of special prayer. It's a way of asking God for a blessing, or of expressing love to Him."

"What are you asking for?"

"Your mother and I are praying for you and your brother, today. We're asking God to lead and direct your lives; we want Him to help you choose a profession and to find the right person to marry, if that is His will. We're also asking Him to walk with you every day of your lives."

"You must love us a lot to fast and pray like that."

"We *do* love you. And God loves you even more."

I suppose there's another explanation behind my concern for the spiritual welfare of our two children. I'm told that George McCluskey, my great-grandfather on the maternal side, carried a similar burden for his children through the final decades of his life. He invested the hour from eleven to twelve o'clock each morning to intercessory prayer for his family. However, he was not only asking God to bless his children; he extended his request to generations not yet born! In effect, my great-grandfather was praying for *me*.

Toward the end of his life, the old man announced that God had made a very unusual promise to him. He was given the assurance that *every* member of four generations of our family would be Christians, including those yet to be born. He then died and the promise became part of the spiritual heritage that was passed to those of us in George McCluskey's bloodline.

Since I represent the fourth generation subsequent to the one that included my great-grandfather, his promise assumes added significance. It has, in fact, been fulfilled in a fascinating way. McCluskey and his wife were ministers and charter members in their church denomination. They brought two daughters into the world, one eventually becoming my grandmother and the other my great-aunt. Those two girls married men who were ministers in the same denomination as their parents. Between them, they produced a boy and four girls, one becoming my mother. The girls all married ministers in the same denomination and the boy became one. Then came my generation. My cousin H. B. London and I were the first two members to reach the age for college, where we were roommates. During the first semester of our sophomore year, he announced that God had called him to be a minister in (you guessed it) the same denomination as his great-grandfather. And believe me, I began to get very *nervous* about the entire proposition!

I now represent the first, though not the only, member of four generations from the time of my great-grandfather who has not felt specifically "called" into the ministry. But considering the hundreds of times I have stood before audiences, talking about the Gospel of Jesus Christ and its application to family life, I have to ask, "What's the difference?"! God has marvelous methods of implementing His purposes in our lives. There have been times as I have sat on the platform of a large church, waiting to speak, that I have felt the presence of the old man . . . and it seemed as though he was smiling mischievously from the beyond.

Though my great-grandfather is long dead, having died a year before my birth, he still provides the richest source of inspiration for me. It staggers the mind to realize that the prayers of this one man, spoken more than fifty years ago, reach across four generations of time and influence developments in my life today. That is the power of prayer and the source of my hope and optimism. Don't tell me God is dead . . . or that He doesn't honor His commitments. George McCluskey and I know that He lives!

The men in my family have transmitted a spiritual heritage that is more valuable than any monetary estate they could have accumulated. And I am determined to preserve it on behalf of my children. There is no higher calling on the face of the earth.

The following prayer was spoken by my father, as part of our wedding ceremony. It made everyone cry.

O eternal God: We bring Thee our children, Jimmy and Shirley. They were Thine but Thou in love didst lend them to us for a little season: to care for, to love and to cherish. It has been a labor of love and has seemed but a few days because of the affection we bear them. Fresh from thy hand they were, in the morning of their lives. Clean and upright, but yet two separate personalities. Tonight we give them back to Thee—no longer as two—but as one flesh. May nothing short of death dissolve the union here cemented. And to this end let the marvelous grace of God do its perfect work!

It is also our earnest prayer for them, not that God shall have a part in their lives, but that He shall have the preeminent part; not that they shall possess faith, but that faith shall fully possess them both; that in a materialistic world they shall not live for the earthly and temporal alone, but that they shall be enabled to lay hold on that which is *spiritual* and *eternal.*

Let their lives together be like the course of the sun: rising in strength, going forth in power and shining more and more unto the perfect day. Let the end of their lives resemble the setting of the sun: going down in a sea of glory, only to shine on undimmed in the firmament of a better world than this.

In the name of the Father, and of the Son and of the Holy Ghost, Amen.

Chapter 6

A Man and His Authority

THE FOLLOWING "Letter to the Editor" appeared in *Moody Monthly*, dated February 1979:

The other day I was sitting in a muffler shop, waiting for a new muffler to be put in our car. A young Mommi came in with Mark, about five years old, and plopped down two seats away from mine. After three minutes, Mark began to demand "a dwink," pointing to the pop machine.

"No, Mark," the Mommi said. But Mark knew, and I knew, by the way she said "no" that she really meant "keep pushing me and I'll give in." So Mark began his campaign. He threatened to hit her. He got on the floor and screamed. He accused her of not loving him. And he said some things that little Maxis or Marks should not say. It was too much.

I turned to the Mommi and said, "Please, for Mark's sake,

discipline him! He will thank you for it later. Buy a copy of Dr. James Dobson's book, *Dare to Discipline* (Tyndale) for Mark's sake and yours."

Did she? I don't know. Will you? I hope so.

The letter was unsigned, so I have no way of thanking the writer for her generous recommendation. I know how she feels, however, for I have also watched little Maxis and Marks do their thing in airports and restaurants and muffler shops across the country. And as you might guess, it is incredibly difficult for me to remain silent when I see a 40-pound child intimidate and outmaneuver his 150-pound parent. I'm rarely as blunt as the writer of the letter above, although I once asked the mother of a four-year-old spitfire named Tara if her child's name was spelled Terror. Mother did not reply.

In the absence of parental leadership, some children become extremely obnoxious and defiant, especially in public places. Perhaps the best example was a ten-year-old boy named Robert, who was a patient of my good friend Dr. William Slonecker. Dr. Slonecker said his pediatric staff dreaded the days when Robert was scheduled for an office visit. He literally attacked the clinic, grabbing instruments and files and telephones. His passive mother could do little more than shake her head in bewilderment.

During one physical examination, Dr. Slonecker observed severe cavities in Robert's teeth and knew that the boy must be referred to a local dentist. But who would be given the honor? A referral like Robert could mean the end of a professional friendship. Dr. Slonecker eventually decided to send him to an older dentist who reportedly understood children. The confrontation that followed now stands as one of the classic moments in the history of human conflict.

Robert arrived in the dental office, prepared for battle.

"Get in the chair, young man," said the doctor.

"No chance!" replied the boy.

"Son, I told you to climb onto the chair, and that's what I intend for you to do," said the dentist.

Robert stared at his opponent for a moment and then replied, "If you make me get in that chair, I will take off all my clothes."

The dentist calmly said, "Son, take 'em off."

The boy forthwith removed his shirt, undershirt, shoes and socks, and then looked up in defiance.

"All right, son," said the dentist. "Now get on the chair."

"You didn't hear me," sputtered Robert. "I said if you make me get on that chair, I will take off *all* my clothes."

"Son, take 'em off," replied the man.

Robert proceeded to removed his pants and shorts, finally standing totally naked before the dentist and his assistant.

"Now, son, get in the chair," said the doctor.

Robert did as he was told, and sat cooperatively through the entire procedure. When the cavities were drilled and filled, he was instructed to step down from the chair.

"Give me my clothes now," said the boy.

"I'm sorry," replied the dentist. "Tell your mother that we're going to keep your clothes tonight. She can pick them up tomorrow."

Can you comprehend the shock Robert's mother received when the door to the waiting room opened, and there stood her pink son, as naked as the day he was born? The room was filled with patients, but Robert and his mom walked past them and into the hall. They went down a public elevator and into the parking lot, ignoring the snickers of onlookers.

The next day, Robert's mother returned to retrieve his clothes, and asked to have a word with the dentist. However, she did not come to protest. These were her sentiments: "You don't know how much I appreciate what happened here yesterday. You see, Robert has been blackmailing me about his clothes for years. Whenever we are in a public place, such as a grocery store, he makes unreasonable demands of me. If I don't immediately buy him what he wants, he threatens to take off all his clothes. You are the first person who has called his bluff, doctor, and the impact on Robert has been incredible!"

No great insight is required to recognize the need for discipline in the lives of Robert, Tara, and Mark, among thousands of their peers. Common sense would reveal as much. Children who are permitted to rule their bewildered parents are among the most frustrated creatures in God's universe, as they scream and protest and pound on the floor. Nevertheless, the humanistic theorists of our day have somehow concluded that what these kids need is freedom from adult leadership. Authority, even when it is permeated with love, is perceived as harmful to children.

That incredible concept has given birth to a powerful political force operating within the Children's Rights Movement (CRM). Their objectives are outlined in a Child's Bill of Rights, originally written by Dr. Richard Farson, * and paraphrased below:

1. Children should have the right to make *all* their own decisions. CRM advocates consider this to be the fundamental right on which all others stand. As such, it proposes the annihilation of parental leadership.

2. Children of any age should have the right to live where they choose. For example, if a three-year-old boy decided to move in with a candy-buying neighbor, his parents would be legally prohibited from bringing him home. No kidding!

3. Children of any age should have the right to vote and be involved in any decisions that affect their lives (whether governmental, ecclesiastical, educational, medical or familial.)

4. Children should have access to any information that is available to adults. No pornography or violence could be shielded from a child, nor could his medical or school records be withheld.

5. Children should be permitted to engage in any sexual

---

* Richard Farson, *Birthrights: A Child's Bill of Rights* (New York: Macmillan, 1974).

activity that is legal for their parents. If a fifteen-year-old boy elected to bring home a playmate to spend the night, his parents could only step aside and watch them shut the bedroom door. An eight-year-old girl could pleasure an adult male with no legal implication for either generation, provided the consent was "mutual."

6. Children of any age should be totally responsible for their own educational pursuits, being free to quit school or attend only when convenient. Compulsory education would be eliminated at all grade levels.

7. Children should have their physical environment constructed to fit their size, instead of asking them to adapt to the world of adults. The meaning of this item is unclear; I'm assuming it would be illegal to build adult-sized furniture or put drinking fountains at their present height.

8. Children should never be spanked under any circumstances, whether at school or at home.

9. Children should be guaranteed the same system of justice that now applies to adults. No minor disciplinary action could occur at school, for example, until the child was tried, faced by his accusers, informed of the evidence against him, and pronounced guilty by a jury of his peers.

10. Children of any age should be permitted to join a labor union, seek employment, receive equal pay for equal work, sign legal contracts, manage all of their own money, and be financially independent. The scrawled signature of a seven-year-old would be legally binding. It has even been suggested by John Holt and others that children should receive a guaranteed income, although it is unclear whom he intended to provide it.

Can there be any doubt about the objective of these extreme "Children's Rights" advocates? They do not wish merely to *weaken* parental authority; they want to *kill* it, once and for all. Their stated goals represent, in essence, a series of prohibitions for parents and teachers. No, sir, you can't require your eight year old to go to school, or live at home, or feed the dog, or attend church, or take his medicine, or speak respectfully to parents, or be home by midnight, or clean his room, or return the stolen toy, or avoid X-rated movies, or stop playing "doctor" with the child next door, or quit drinking liquor. No, sir, you will go to jail if you deprive your child of his rights in this fashion. You are the "peer" of your son, not his leader.

"Talk is cheap," I can hear a few readers saying. "Just because a kookie psychologist offers some way-out proposals for children is no reason to believe those restrictions will be imposed on *my* family."

I'm not so confident. The first major triumph for CRM was achieved in Sweden, 1979, when it became illegal for parents to spank or otherwise punish their children. The law, which the Swedish Parliament passed by a vote of 259–6, prohibits "*any* act which, for the purpose of punishing, causes the child injury or pain, even if the disturbance is mild and passing." The intent also prohibits psychological punishment such as scoldings, sending the child to the bedroom, withdrawing television rights, and similar humiliations. An emergency telephone service is provided twenty-four hours a day so that youngsters can report parental violations directly to an ombudsman.

Following this incredible development, American psychologists took to the airways, advocating passage of a similar law in this country. The elimination of punishment is merely a small part of what the *Los Angeles Times* called "The Mounting March for Children's Rights." Accordingly, we can expect the other nine objectives to become increasingly volatile in the years ahead. In Sweden, again, where the Movement has found the most fertile ground, a prominent professor of law at Stockholm University has proposed that the Swedish constitution be amended to provide numerous rights to minors. One component that he hopes to include is the right of kids to "divorce" their parents. (Since writing the statement above, Sweden *has* passed the proposed law.)

I should emphasize that I am not opposed to the many worthwhile organizations that are working to secure a better life for children. Physical abuse, sexual exploitation, and psychological trauma are being inflicted on helpless boys and girls across this country, and I certainly do not wish to discredit the efforts of those who seek to ameliorate their suffering. However, within this body of concerned individuals is a smaller constituency which I have described. They seek to impose a new way of life . . . a new parental ethic . . . on families everywhere. They apparently wish to replace the ancient wisdom of the Judeo-Christian philosophy with the humanistic notions of the twentieth century. They have been remarkably successful in this effort during the past decade.

The extreme element of the Children's Rights Movement is now shifting its emphasis from a philosophical level to the courtroom. Only last month I received a letter from an attorney who sought my help in defending a father who was threatened with the loss of his child. The details are difficult to believe. It appears that the Department of Social Service in his community is attempting to remove a six-year-old girl from her home because her father will not permit her to attend movies, listen to rock music or watch certain television programs. This child is well adjusted emotionally and is popular with her friends in school. Her teacher reports that she ranks in the top five students in her class, academically. Nevertheless, the courts are being asked to remove her from her home because of the intolerable "abuse" she is experiencing there.

Few matters make me angry during this tranquil phase of my life, but you've just read one of them. When humanists are permitted to impose their naive idealism on the composition and functioning of the basic family unit, including yours and mine, then we are in serious trouble as a nation. In this instance, they are undermining the right of parents to instill moral values in their children, which is a responsibility ordained by God, Himself. I have written these words before, but feel compelled to repeat their beleaguered message: authority is the glue that holds human organizations together, whether in a government, military, school, business . . . or home. Without leadership in human relationships, chaos soon reigns supreme.

Three principles relative to authority are vitally important to the family, and to the continuation of our way of life. Let me discuss them briefly:

1. The primary responsibility for the provision of authority in the home has been assigned to men.

It will not be popular to restate the age-old Biblical concept that God holds *men* accountable for leadership in their families. Nevertheless, that's the way I interpret the Scriptures. 1 Timothy 3:4–5 (PHILLIPS) states:

> He [the father] must have proper authority in his own household, and be able to control and command the respect of his children.

Whether women's activists like it or not, a Christian man is obligated to lead his family to the best of his ability. This assignment does not justify iron-fisted oppression of children or the disregard of a woman's needs and wishes, of course. But God apparently expects a *man* to be the ultimate decision maker in his family. Likewise, he bears heavier responsibility for the outcome of those decisions. If his family has purchased too many items on credit, then the financial crunch is ultimately his fault. If the family never reads the Bible or seldom goes to church on Sunday, God holds the man to blame. If the children are disrespectful and disobedient, the primary responsibility lies with the father . . . not his wife. (I don't remember Eli's wife being criticized for raising two evil sons; it was her husband who came under God's wrath. See 1 Samuel 3:13.)

From this perspective, what happens to a family when the designated leader doesn't do his job? Similar consequences can be seen in a corporation whose president only pretends to direct the company. The organization disintegrates very quickly. The parallel to leaderless families is too striking to be missed. In my view, America's greatest need is for husbands to begin guiding their families, rather than pouring every physical and emotional resource into the mere acquisition of money. That belief motivated the book you are reading.

2. Children naturally look to their fathers for authority.

When my son Ryan was five years old, he overheard a reference to my childhood.

"Daddy, were you ever a little boy?" he asked.

"Yes, Ryan, I was smaller than you," I replied.

"Were you ever a *baby?*" he inquired with disbelief.

"Yes. Everyone is a tiny baby when he is born."

Ryan looked puzzled. He simply could not comprehend his 6-foot 2-inch, 190-pound father as an infant. He thought for a minute and then said, "Were you a *daddy*-baby?"

It was impossible for Ryan to imagine me without the mantle of authority, even if I were a tiny newborn. His nine-year-old sister reacted similarly the first time she was shown home movies of me when I was only four. There on the screen was a baby-faced, innocent lad on a horse. Danae had to be assured that the picture was of me, whereupon she exclaimed, "*That* kid spanks me?!"

Danae and Ryan both revealed their perception of me . . . not as a man who had been given authority . . . but as a man who *was* authority. Such is the nature of childhood. Boys and girls typically look to their fathers, whose size and power and deeper voices bespeak leadership. That's why, despite numerous exceptions, men teachers are likely to handle classroom discipline more easily than soft ladies with feminine voices. (A woman teacher once told me that the struggle to control her class was like trying to keep thirty-two Ping-Pong balls under water at the same time.)

That is also why mothers need the disciplinary involvement of their husbands. Not that a man must handle every act of disobedience, but he should serve as the frame on which parental authority is constructed. Furthermore, it must be clear to the kids that Dad is in agreement with Mother's policies and he will defend her in instances of insurrection. Referring to 1 Timothy again, this is what is meant by a father having the "proper authority in his own household."

3. Authority *will* be tested.

Deeply ingrained in the human temperament is a self-will that rejects external authority. This spirit of rebellion manifests itself during the first year of life and dominates the personality during the second. The "terrible twos" can be summarized by this barbed question, "By what right do you or anyone else try to tell me what to do with my life!?" That same question will be bellowed during the adolescent years, along with sweet little comments such as, "I didn't ask to be born, you know!" Johnny Carson once said that if his teenager ever said that to him he'd reply, "It's a good thing you didn't ask. I'd have said *no.*"

My point is that human beings at all ages are inclined to test the limits of authority. At its most basic level, this resistance is an expression of mankind's spiritual rebellion against God. Anyone who doubts this stubborn nature need only observe the sheer power of a toddler's self-will. Have you ever seen an angry three year old hold his breath until he becomes unconscious? It happens. Consider the child whose mother wrote me the following note:

My husband and I realized our two-year-old daughter was a strong-willed child the night she was introduced to green peas. Julie took one bite and then refused to swallow. But she also refused to spit out the peas, no matter what we tried to do. We attempted to pry open her jaws, then threatened to spank her. Finally, we pleaded with Julie to cooperate, but she wouldn't budge. There was nothing left to do but put her to bed. Twelve hours later she awoke bright and cheery with no peas in her mouth. We found them in a little pile down at the foot of her bed. Her father and I were very relieved that those green peas did not remain in her mouth all night long!

Could it be that a two-year-old girl is actually capable of outmaneuvering and outlasting the adults in her world? It certainly is. And if there is one blind spot in twentieth-century psychology, it is the failure to recognize this pugnacious human temperament and the importance of responding appropriately when willful defiance occurs.

But what is the appropriate action to take in moments of rebellion? I will permit a Certified Public Accountant, William Jarnagin, to answer that question. He recently wrote me the following letter which speaks volumes about parent-child relationships.

Dear Dr. Dobson:

This is a note of thanks for your work in strengthening the American family. My wife and I have recently read four of your books and we have profited very much from them.

Please permit me to relate a recent experience with our six-year-old son, David. Last Friday night, my wife, Becky, told him to pick up some orange peelings he had left on the carpet, which he knows is a "no-no." He failed to respond, and as a result received one slap on his behind, whereupon he began an obviously defiant temper tantrum.

Since I had observed the whole episode, I then called for my paddle and applied it appropriately, saw to it that he picked up and properly disposed of the orange peelings, and sent him straight to bed, since it was already past his bedtime. After a few minutes, when his emotions had had a chance to settle down, I went to his room and explained that God had instructed all parents who truly love their children to properly discipline them, etc., and that we truly love him and therefore would not permit such defiant behavior.

The next morning, after I had gone to work, David presented his mother with the following letter, together with a little stack of ten pennies:

From David and Deborah
To Mom and Dad

Ross Dr. 3d house
Sellmer, Tennasse
39718

Dear Mom and Dad

here is 10 Cints for
Pattelling me when I
really neded and that
gos for Deborah to   I
love you

Love yur son David
and yur Doter Deborah

Oh, incidentally, Deborah is our one-year-old daughter whose adoption should be final sometime in June.

Keep up your good work and may God bless you.

Sincerely,
William H. Jarnagin

Mr. William Jarnagin understands the appropriate response of a father to a child's defiance. It is neither harsh nor insulting nor dangerous nor whimsical. Rather, it represents the firm but loving discipline that is required for the best interest of the child. How fortunate is the boy or girl whose father still comprehends that timeless concept.

Summary

American men have experienced a severe crisis of identity in recent years, similar to the confusion that their wives have encountered. It has been brought on by persistent challenges to everything traditionally masculine, just as the women's movement has mocked traditionally female behavior and mores. Masculine leadership, especially, has been ridiculed as "macho" and invariably self-serving. But the purpose of this chapter has been to reaffirm the importance of authority in a family—first, in the provision of gentle direction and guidance, and second, in raising healthy children. Both objectives appear to be part of the Creator's blueprint for a successful home.

Chapter 7

Questions Pertaining to Children

W E HAVE DEALT exclusively with the relationship between a man and his children to this point. Before turning to other aspects of masculine involvement, perhaps we should devote a remaining chapter to questions and answers relevant to boys and girls. This approach will permit me to clarify the views presented, while anticipating additional questions that might have been raised. Of special concern will be the matter of man's "ultimate priority"—winning children to Christ.

We'll begin with an issue that is especially troubling to Christian women, today. It is, in fact, a question that is often asked whenever I speak on the subject of fatherhood.

1. *I agree with your belief that the father should be the spiritual leader in the family, but it just doesn't happen that way at our house. If*

the kids go to church on Sunday, it's because I wake them up and
see that they get ready. If we have family devotions, it's done at my
insistence, and I'm the one who prays with the children at bedtime.
If I didn't do these things, our kids would have no spiritual training.
Nevertheless, people keep saying that I should wait for my husband
to accept spiritual leadership in our family. What do you advise in
my situation?

That's an extremely important question, and a subject of
controversy right now. As you indicated, some Christian leaders
instruct women to wait passively for their husbands to assume
spiritual responsibility. Until that leadership is accepted, they
recommend that wives stay out of the way and let God put
pressure on the husband to assume the role that He's given to
men. I strongly disagree with that view when small children are
involved. If the issue focused only on the spiritual welfare of a
husband and wife, then a woman could afford to bide her time.
However, the presence of boys and girls changes the picture
dramatically. Every day that goes by without spiritual training
for them is a day that can never be recaptured.

Therefore, if your husband is not going to accept the role of
spiritual leadership that God has given him, then I believe you
must do it. You have no time to lose. You should continue
taking the family to church on Sunday. You should pray with
the children and teach them to read the Bible. Furthermore,
you must continue your private devotions and maintain your
own relationship with God. In short, I feel that the spiritual life
of children (and adults) is simply too important for a woman to
postpone for two or four or six years, hoping her husband will
eventually awaken. Jesus made it clear that members of our own
family can erect the greatest barriers to our faith, but must not
be permitted to do so. He says, "Do not think that I have come
to bring peace on earth; I have not come to bring peace, but a
sword. For I have come to set a man against his father, and a
daughter against her mother, and a daughter-in-law against her

mother-in-law; and a man's foes will be those of his own household. He who loves father or mother more than me is not worthy of me; and he who loves son or daughter more than me is not worthy of me" (Matt. 10:34–38, RSV).

I mentioned my grandfather, R. L. Dobson, earlier in this book. He was a moral man who saw no need for the Christian faith. His spiritual disinterest placed my grandmother, Juanita Dobson, under great pressure, for she was a devout Christian who felt she must put God first. Therefore, she accepted the responsibility of introducing her six children to Jesus Christ. There were times when my grandfather exerted tremendous pressure on her, not to give up her faith, but to leave him out of it.

He said, "I am a good father and provider, I pay my bills, and I am honest in dealing with my fellow man. That is enough."

His wife replied, "You are a good man, but that is *not* enough. You should give your heart to God." This he could not comprehend.

My 97-pound grandmother made no attempt to force her faith on her husband, nor did she treat him disrespectfully. But she quietly continued to pray and fast for the man she loved. For more than forty years she brought this same petition before God on her knees.

Then at sixty-nine years of age, my grandfather suffered a stroke, and for the first time in his life he was desperately ill. One day his young daughter came into his room to clean and straighten. As she walked by his bed, she saw tears in his eyes. No one had ever seen him cry before.

"Daddy, what's wrong?" she asked.

He responded, "Honey, go to the head of the stairs and call your mother."

My grandmother ran to her husband's side and heard him say, "I know I'm going to die and I'm not afraid of death, but it's so dark. There's no way out. I've lived my whole life through and missed the one thing that really matters. Will you pray for me?"

"Will I pray?" exclaimed my grandmother. She had been hoping for that request throughout her adult life. She fell to her knees and the intercessions of forty years seemed to pour out through that bedside prayer. R. L. Dobson gave his heart to God that day in a wonderful way.

During the next two weeks, he asked to see some of the church people whom he had offended and requested their forgiveness. He concluded his personal affairs and then died with a testimony on his lips. Before descending into a coma from which he would never awaken, my grandfather said, " . . . Now there is a way through the darkness."

The unrelenting prayers of my little grandmother had been answered.

Returning to the question, I would like to caution women not to become "self-righteous" and critical of their husbands. Let everything be done in a spirit of love. However, there may be some lonely years when the burden of spiritual leadership with children must be carried alone. If that is the case, the Lord has promised to walk with you through these difficult days.

2. *Parents have been commanded in the Bible to "train up a child in the way he should go." But this poses a critical question: What way should he go? If the first seven years represent the "prime time" for religious training, what should be taught during this period? What experiences should be included? What values should be emphasized?*

It is my strong belief that a child should be exposed to a carefully conceived, systematic program of religious training. Yet we are much too haphazard about this matter. Perhaps we would hit the mark more often if we more clearly recognized the precise target.

Listed below is a "Checklist for Spiritual Training"—a set of targets at which to aim. Many of the items require maturity which children lack, and we should not try to make adult

Christians out of our immature youngsters. But we can gently urge them toward these goals—these targets—during the impressionable years of childhood.

Essentially, the five scriptural concepts which follow should be consciously taught, providing the foundation on which all future doctrine and faith will rest. I encourage every Christian parent to evaluate his child's understanding of these five areas:

CONCEPT I: "And thou shalt love the Lord thy God with all thy heart" (Mark 12:30, KJV).
1. Is your child learning of the love of God through the love, tenderness, and mercy of his parents? (most important)
2. Is he learning to talk about the Lord, and to include Him in his thoughts and plans?
3. Is he learning to turn to Jesus for help whenever he is frightened or anxious or lonely?
4. Is he learning to read the Bible?
5. Is he learning to pray?
6. Is he learning the meaning of faith and trust?
7. Is he learning the joy of the Christian way of life?
8. Is he learning the beauty of Jesus' birth and death?

CONCEPT II: "Thou shalt love thy neighbor as thyself" (Mark 12:31, KJV).
1. Is he learning to understand and empathize with the feelings of others?
2. Is he learning not to be selfish and demanding?
3. Is he learning to share?
4. Is he learning not to gossip and criticize others?
5. Is he learning to accept himself?

CONCEPT III: "Teach me to do thy will; for thou art my God" (Ps. 143:10, KJV).
1. Is he learning to obey his parents as preparation for later obedience to God? (most important)
2. Is he learning to behave properly in church—God's house?

3. Is he learning a healthy appreciation for both aspects of God's nature: love and justice?
4. Is he learning that there are many forms of benevolent authority outside himself to which he must submit?
5. Is he learning the meaning of sin and its inevitable consequences?

CONCEPT IV: "Fear God, and keep his commandments: for this is the whole duty of man" (Eccles. 12:13, KJV).
1. Is he learning to be truthful and honest?   *O.T.*
2. Is he learning to keep the Sabbath day holy?   *we keep Sunday*
3. Is he learning the relative insignificance of materialism?
4. Is he learning the meaning of the Christian family, and the faithfulness to it which God intends?
5. Is he learning to follow the dictates of his own conscience?

CONCEPT V: "But the fruit of the Spirit is . . . self-control" (Gal. 5:22–23, RSV).
1. Is he learning to give a portion of his allowance (and other money) to God?
2. Is he learning to control his impulses?
3. Is he learning to work and carry responsibility?
4. Is he learning the vast difference between self-worth and egotistical pride?
5. Is he learning to bow in reverence before the God of the universe?

In summary, your child's first seven years should prepare him to say, at the age of accountability, "Here am I, Lord, Send me!"

3. *It is very difficult for us to have meaningful devotions as a family because our young children seem so bored and uninvolved. They yawn and squirm and giggle while we are reading the Bible. On the other hand, we feel it is important to teach them to pray and study God's word. Can you help us deal with this dilemma?*

The one key word to family devotions is *brevity*. Children can't be expected to comprehend and appreciate lengthy adult spiritual activities. Four or five minutes devoted to one or two Bible verses, followed by a short prayer, usually represents the limits of attention during the preschool years. To force young children to comprehend eternal truths in an eternal devotional can be eternally dangerous.

4. *My wife and I are new Christians, and we now realize that we raised our kids by the wrong principles. They're grown now, but we continue to worry about the past, and we feel great regret for our failures as parents. Is there anything we can do at this late date?*

Let me deal, first, with the awful guilt you are obviously carrying. There's hardly a parent alive who does not have some regrets and painful memories of their failures as a mother or a father. Children are infinitely complex, and we cannot be perfect parents any more than we can be perfect human beings. The pressures of living are often enormous, and we get tired and irritated; we are influenced by our physical bodies and our emotions, which sometimes prevent us from saying the right things and being the model we should. We don't always handle our children as unemotionally as we wish we had, and it's very common to look back a year or two later and see how wrong we were in the way we approached a problem.

All of us experience these failures! *No one does the job perfectly!* That's why each of us should get alone with the Creator of parents and children, saying,

"Lord, you know my inadequacies. You know my weaknesses, not only in parenting, but in every area of my life. I did the best I could, but it wasn't good enough. As You broke the fishes and the loaves to feed the five thousand, now take my meager effort and use it to bless my family. Make up for the things I did wrong. Satisfy the needs that I have not satisfied. Wrap your great arms around my children, and draw them close to you. And be there when they stand at the great crossroads between right and wrong. All I can give is my best, and I've done that. Therefore, I submit to you my children and my self and the job I did as a parent. The outcome now belongs to you."

I know God will honor that prayer, even for parents whose job is finished. The Lord does not want you to suffer from guilt over events you can no longer influence. The past is the past. Let it die never to be resurrected. Give the situation to God, and let Him have it. I think you'll be surprised to learn that you're no longer alone!

5. *My wife and I are extremely busy during this period of our lives. My job takes me on the road several days a week, and my wife has become very successful as a real estate agent. Quite honestly, we are not able to spend much time with our three children, but we give them our undivided attention when we are together. My wife and I wish we had more family time, but we take comfort in knowing that it's not the quantity of time between parent and child that really matters; it's the quality of that time that makes the difference. Would you agree with that statement?*

Permit me to respond to your question by a back-door approach which may seem irrelevant, at first. As a person who earns part of his living by use of the King's English, I often find myself examining the validity of folk wisdom and clichés which have been accepted prima facie within our culture. While discussing the legal ramifications of pornography with a friend, for example, he confidently uttered that familiar phrase, "Well, you can't legislate morality, you know." I nodded in agreement, but later asked myself, "Why not?"

It is immoral to kill, rape, slander, defraud, and plunder, yet we have managed to legislate against these behaviors, haven't we? Is not all criminal law based on the prohibition of certain inherently evil acts? Indeed, we would be in a mess if our lawmakers truly believed, "You can't legislate morality, you know."

Returning to the question of quantity versus quality in parent child relationships, we confront yet another widely quoted cliché that is equally porous. Without intending disrespect for the father who asked the above question, this phrase is bandied about by overcommitted and harassed parents who feel guilty about the lack of time they spend with their children. Their boys and girls are parked at child care centers during the day and with baby sitters at night, leaving little time for traditional parenting activities. And to handle the discomfort of neglecting their children, Mom and Dad cling to a catch-phrase that makes it seem so healthy and proper: "Well, you know, it's not the *quantity* of time that matters, it's the *quality* of your togetherness that counts."

There is a grain of truth in most popular notions, and this one is no exception. We can all agree that there is no benefit in being with our children seven days a week if we are angry, oppressive, unnurturing and capricious with them. But from that point forward, the quantity versus quality issue runs aground. Simply stated, *that dichotomy will not be tolerated in any other area of our lives; why do we apply it only to children?* Let me illustrate.

Let's suppose you are very hungry, having eaten nothing all day. You select the best restaurant in your city and ask the waiter for the finest steak on his menu. He replies that the filet mignon is the house favorite, and you order it charcoal-broiled, medium rare. The waiter returns twenty minutes later with the fare and sets it before you. There in the center of a large plate is a lonely piece of meat, one inch square, flanked by a single bite of potato.

You complain vigorously to the waiter. "Is this what you call a steak dinner?"

He then replies, "Sir, how can you criticize us before you taste that meat? I have brought you one square inch of the finest steak money can buy. It is cooked to perfection, salted with care, and served while hot. In fact, I doubt if you could get a better piece of meat anywhere in the city. I'll admit that the serving is small, but after all, sir, everyone knows that it isn't the quantity that matters; it's the quality that counts in steak dinners."

"Nonsense!" you reply, and I certainly agree. You see, the subtlety of this simple phrase is that it pits two necessary virtues in opposition to one another and invites us to choose between them. If quantity and quality are worthwhile ingredients in family relationships, then why not give our kids *both?* It is insufficient to toss our "hungry" children an occasional bite of steak, even if it is prime, corn-fed filet mignon.

My concern is that the quantity versus quality cliché has become, perhaps, a rationalization for giving our kids *neither!*

6. *I want to ask you a very personal question. Your books deal with practical aspects of everyday living. They offer solutions and suggestions for handling the typical frustrations and problems of parenthood and marriage. But that makes me wonder about your own family. Does your home always run smoothly? Do you ever feel like a failure as a father? And if so, how do you deal with self-doubt and recrimination?*

I have been asked this question many times, although the answer should surprise no one. Shirley and I experience the same frustrations and pressures that others face. Our behavior is not always exemplary, nor is that of our children. And our household can become very hectic at times.

Perhaps I can best illustrate my reply by describing the day we now refer to as "Black Sunday." For some reason, the Sabbath (Saturday) can be the most frustrating day of the week for us, especially during the morning hours. I've found that other parents also experience tensions during the "get 'em ready for church" routine. But Black Sunday was especially chaotic. We began that day by getting up too late, meaning everyone had to rush to get to church on time. That produced emotional pressure, especially for Shirley and me. Then there was the matter of the spilt milk at breakfast, and the black shoe polish on the floor. And, of course, Ryan got dressed first, enabling him to slip out the back door and get himself dirty from head to toe. It was necessary to take him down to the skin and start over with clean clothes once more. Instead of handling these irritants as they arose, we began criticizing one another and hurling accusations back and forth. At least one spanking was delivered, as I recall, and another three or four were promised. Yes, it was a day to be remembered (or forgotten). Finally, four harried people managed to stumble into church, ready for a great spiritual blessing, no doubt. There's not a pastor in the world who could have moved us on that morning.

I felt guilty throughout the day for the strident tone of our home on that Black Sunday. Sure, our children shared the blame, but they were merely responding to our disorganization. Shirley and I had overslept, and that's where the conflict originated.

After the evening service, I called the family together around the kitchen table. I began by describing the kind of day we had had, and asked each person to forgive me for my part in it. Furthermore, I said that I thought we should give each member of the family an opportunity to say whatever he or she was feeling inside.

Ryan was given the first shot, and he fired it at his mother.

"You've been a real grouch today, Mom!" he said with feeling. "You've blamed me for everything I've done all day long."

Shirley then explained why she had been unhappy with her son, trying not to be defensive about his charges.

Danae then poured out her hostilities and frustrations. Finally, Shirley and I had an opportunity to explain the tensions that had caused our overreaction.

It was a valuable time of ventilation and honesty that drew us together once more. We then had prayer as a family and asked the Lord to help us live and work together in love and harmony.

My point is that *every* family has moments when they violate all the rules—even departing from the Christian principles by which they have lived. Fatigue itself can damage all the high ideals which have been recommended to parents in seminars and books and sermons. The important question is, how do mothers and fathers reestablish friendship within their families when the storm has passed? Open, nonthreatening discussion offers one solution to that situation.

Returning to the question, let's acknowledge that a psychologist can no more prevent all emotional distress for his family than a physician can circumvent disease in his. We live in an imperfect world which inflicts struggles on us all. Nevertheless, Biblical principles offer the most healthy approach to family living—even turning stress to our advantage. (Someday I'll tell you about Black Monday.)

7. *You've indicated that seven deaths have occurred in your family during the past eighteen months. We have also had several tragic losses in our family in recent years. My wife died when our children were five, eight, and nine. I found it very difficult to explain death to them during that time. Can you offer some guidelines regarding how a parent can help his children cope with the stark reality of death—especially when it strikes within the immediate family?*

Some years ago, I attended a funeral at the Inglewood Cemetery-Mortuary in Inglewood, California. While there, I picked up a brochure written by the president of the mortuary, John M. McKinley. Mr. McKinley had been in the funeral business for fifteen years before writing this valuable pamphlet entitled "If It Happens To Your Child." He gave me permission to reproduce the content here in answer to your question.

I knew Tommy's parents because they lived in the neighborhood and attended the same church. But I knew Tommy especially well because he was one of the liveliest, happiest five-year-olds it had ever been my pleasure to meet. It was a shock, therefore, when his mother became a client of mine at the death of her husband.

As a doctor must learn to protect himself from the suffering of his patients, so a funeral director must protect himself from grief. During the course of the average year I come in direct contact with several thousand men and women who have experienced a shattering loss, and if I did not isolate myself from their emotions, my job would be impossible. But I have not been able to isolate myself from the children.

"I don't know what I would have done if I had not had Tommy," his mother told me when I visited her in her home the morning she called me. "He has been such a little man—hasn't cried, and is doing everything he can to take his daddy's place." And it was true. Tommy was standing just as he imagined a man would stand, not crying, and doing his best to take his daddy's place.

I knew it was wrong. I knew I should tell her so—that Tommy was not a man; that he needed to cry; that he needed comfort probably far more than she. But I am not a psychologist, and I said nothing.

In the two years since then I have watched Tommy. The joy has not come back in his face, and it is clear even to my layman's mind that he is an emotionally sick child. I am sure it began when his mother, unknowingly, made it difficult—impossible—for him to express his grief, and placed on him an obligation he could not fulfill; that of "taking daddy's place."

There have been few examples so clear cut as Tommy's, but I have seen so much that made me wince, and I have been asked so often: "What should I tell Mary?" or Paul, or Jim, that I finally decided to do something about it. I went to the experts, the men who know how a child should be treated at such moments of tragedy, and I asked them to lay down some guidelines that parents could understand and follow. I talked to several psychologists and psychiatrists and pediatricians, but principally to Dr. A. I. Duvall, a psychiatrist, and Dr. James Gardner, a child psychologist. Translated into my layman's language, here is the gist of what I learned:

—When a child, like any other human being, experiences a deeply painful loss, not only should he be permitted to cry; he should be encouraged to cry until the need for tears is gone. He should be comforted while the tears are flowing, but the words "don't cry" should be stricken from the language.

—The need to cry may be recurrent for several days, or at widening intervals, several months; but when the need is felt, no effort should be made to dam the tears. Instead, it should be made clear that it is good to cry, and not "babyish," or "sissy" or anything to be ashamed of.

—At times, the child may need to be alone with his grief, and if this feeling comes, it should be respected. But otherwise physical contact and comfort will be almost as healing as the tears.

—The child should be told the truth; that death is final. "Mommy has gone on a vacation," or "Daddy has gone on a trip" only adds to the confusion and delays the inevitable. Children— particularly young children—have a very imperfect time sense. If "Mommy has gone on a vacation," they are going to expect her back this afternoon or tomorrow. And when tomorrow and tomorrow comes and she does not reappear, not only will the hurt be repeated, endlessly, the child will lose faith in the surviving parent just at the time when faith and trust are needed most. It is hard to say "never" when you know it will make the tears flow harder, but it is the kindest word in the long run.

—It is not necessary to explain death to a young child. It may even be harmful to try. To the five-year-old, "death" is absence, and explanations may only confuse him. If he has seen a dead bird or a dead pet, it may be helpful to make a comparison; but the important fact which the child must accept is absence. If he can be helped to accept the fact that father or mother or brother or sister is gone and will never return, then through questions and observations he will gradually build his own picture of "death" and its meaning.

—A child should not be unduly shielded from the physical appearance and fact of death. If a father dies, the child should be permitted to see the body, so that with his own eyes he can see the changes, the stillness, the difference between the vital strength which was "daddy" and this inanimate mask which is not "daddy" at all. Seeing with his own eyes will help.

—A child should be protected, however, from any massed demonstrations of grief, as from a large group of mourners at a funeral. Rather, the child should be taken in privately before the funeral to say goodbye.

—If the child is very young—say two to five or six—great care should be used in explaining death in terms which are meaningful to adults, but which may be very puzzling to children. For example, to say that "Mommy has gone to Heaven" may make perfect sense to a religious bereaved father, but it may leave a five-year-old wondering why mommy has deserted him. At that answer, "Heaven" is simply a far place, and he will not be able to understand why his mother stays there instead of coming home to take care of him.

—Along with tears, a child is quite likely to feel sharp resentment, even anger at the dead parent, or the brother or sister who has "gone." This feeling is the result of the child's conviction that he has been deserted. If this feeling does arise, the child should be permitted to express it freely, just as in the case of tears.

—More common, and frequently more unsettling to a child is its guilt feelings when a death occurs. If he has been angry at his sister, and the sister dies, he is likely to think it is his fault, that his anger killed her. Or if his mother dies, and he is not told honestly and simply what has happened, he is likely to believe that his misbehavior drove her away. Guilt feelings in young children, reinforced by death, can lead to neurotic patterns which last throughout life.

But if a child is encouraged to cry until the need for tears is gone; if he is comforted enough; if he is told the simple truth; if he is permitted to see for himself the difference between death and life; if his resentment or guilt is handled in the same straightforward way as his tears, his sense of loss will still be great, but he will overcome it.

There is a positive side, too. If death is treated as a natural part of human experience, it is much easier for a loved one to live in memory. When the initial impact of grief is gone, it is a natural thing to remember and re-tell stories which evoke vivid recollections of the personality and habits which made the loved one a special person. Children take great delight in this, for in their rich world of imagination they can make the absent one live again. Such reminiscing does not renew or increase their sorrow. To the extent that it makes them free to remember, the cause for sorrow is removed.

Mr. McKinley's advice is excellent, as far as it goes. However, it has not included any references to the Christian message, which provides the *only* satisfactory answer to death. Obviously, I disagree with Mr. McKinley's reservations about heaven. We can say, "Your mother is gone for now, but thank God we'll be together again on the other side!" How comforting for a grieving child to know that a family reunion will someday occur from which there will never be another separation! I recommend that Christian parents begin acquainting their children with the gift of eternal life long before they have need of this understanding.

8. *A note from the author: One of the great privileges of my life has been the receipt of personal mail from people who have read my books or heard my broadcasts. We receive up to three hundred letters daily, which represent a source of continual enlightenment and encouragement to me. (I read them while riding an exercycle every morning.) Of this mail, the portion I enjoy most comes from children and teenagers. I've reproduced below three letters from kids, because of the unique messages they contain. The final two are examples of many wherein children express frustration regarding their parents' overcommitted schedules.*

Dear Sir:

In your last Newsletter you asked me to help support your television project. I'm writing to let you know why I won't. First, we don't even have a T.V. Second, we send our extra money to Missionaries. Third, I'm only eleven years old and I don't have any money.

Now I want to go back to the first reason, because it is the most important one. In Psalms 101:3 it says: "I will set no wicked thing before my eyes . . ." I have never lived with a television. My parents never bought one. But from reading and hearing other people talk, I understand there are people shown on television who don't have enough clothes on. People who steal, kill, lie and cheat and swear. My parents have taught me, and the Bible says, those things are wicked.

Maybe this doesn't make sense to you, but it does to me. I don't think I'm missing anything, because we get to travel a lot and read lots and lots of books.

Yours truly,
Tanya

Dear Tanya:

Your letter makes plenty of sense to me! Your parents are absolutely right in saying that television is an evil force in our society, and I respect them for having the courage not to own a set.

But I respect *you* even more. At only eleven years of age, you already know what you believe and are committed to the Christian way of life. I only wish most adults had the faith that you revealed in your letter.

God has a purpose for your life, Tanya. It will be fun watching His plan unfold. He loves you very much, and so do I.

James Dobson

Dear Dr. Dobson:

I feel like I've known you all my life after reading *Preparing for Adolescence.* You answered all my questions in it.

I would like to tell you something about my experiences. When I was only seven, we had to move from our town because my dad felt God calling him to the pastorate.

I had always been close to my parents. Then we moved and everything changed. My mom worked longer hours than before. Sometimes I would go a whole week without seeing her. And that's no lie. She would come home crabby and then everybody would go to bed crabby.

My dad was going to seminary, so he had the same schedule as my sister [five years old] and I. But he was studying during his wakeful hours. I thank God for keeping his hand on my sister's and my life during those tender years.

When I was nine years old, my dad was called to be a pastor of a church. Now, three years later, I still have a communication gap with my parents. But not my Heavenly Father.

The first year we were in our new town, I began having severe pains in my legs. Then I couldn't walk. I have juvenile rheumatoid arthritis. Two months later, I was able to walk again, only because of treatments and prayers.

Now I'm starting the seventh grade in September. I still have arthritis but I'm "Learning to Lean."

Please pray for me, Dr. Dobson, as I'm entering adolescence and coping with my arthritis. It still gives me problems with my walking.

Yours in Christ,
Charlotte

Dear Charlotte:

How special it was for you to write me. I receive thousands of letters each year from parents and teachers who have read my books, but fewer young people like you take the time to write. I appreciated your comments about *Preparing for Adolescence,* and I'm glad you found it helpful.

You are obviously a *very* courageous girl and I admire the way you have faced difficult experiences. Remain true and faithful to God's laws, Charlotte, regardless of what the rest of the world does. He will lead and guide you in the important days ahead.

Thanks again for taking time to write and share with me. I know God will continue to bless you as you grow in His love.

Sincerely,
James Dobson

Dear Dr. Dobson

I have a working mom and a working dad and I would like to know what us kids can do.

Brian

I will permit America's parents to respond to Brian's question. They are, after all, the only ones who *can* provide a satisfactory answer to it.

SECTION III

A MAN AND HIS WIFE

Chapter 8

A Man and His Wife

WE TURN OUR attention now to the relationship between husbands and wives, which reminds me of a telephone call I received recently from a man who had read my previous book *The Strong-Willed Child*. It did not answer his questions. Furthermore, he said he had read my earlier book *What Wives Wish Their Husbands Knew About Women*, and it didn't satisfy his needs, either.

"What I want you to write," he continued, "is a combination of those two books on the subject "How To Live With A Strong-Willed Woman"!

I told him I wouldn't touch that topic with a shovel, yet here I am about to wade into an equally volatile matter. I want to discuss the characteristic of women that men complain about most, and vice versa. In fact, I plan to speak more bluntly in

91

this chapter than in any statement I've every written. That should be enough to win me some enemies among both sexes, but the time has come for straight talk to husbands and wives.

Perhaps you know that the divorce rate in America is now higher than in any other civilized nation in the world, and it is steadily increasing. That is tragic. Even more distressing to me is knowledge that the divorce rate for *Christians* is only slightly lower than for the population at large. How could that possibly be true? Jesus taught his followers to be loving, giving, moral, responsible, self-disciplined, honest, and respectful. He also explicitly prohibited divorce except for radical circumstances of infidelity. With these instructions, He provided an unshakable foundation for a stable and loving relationship between husband and wife. How can it be, then, that those who claim to have accepted Jesus' teaching and devoted their lives to Christian principles are hardly more successful in maintaining harmonious families than those who profess nothing? There's an enormous contradiction tucked within those words. As Howard Hendrix said, "If your Christianity doesn't work at home, it doesn't work. Don't export it!"

The truth is, the *same* circumstances that destroy non-Christian marriages can also be deadly in the homes of believers. I'm not referring to alcoholism or infidelity or compulsive gambling. The most common marriage killer is much more subtle and insidious. Let me explain.

Suppose I have a counseling appointment at four o'clock tomorrow afternoon with a person whom I've never met. Who is that person and what will be the complaint that brings them to me? First, the patient will probably be Mrs. Jones, not her husband. A man is seldom the first to seek marriage counseling, and when he does, it is for a different motive than his wife seeks it. She comes because her marriage is driving her crazy. He comes because his *wife* is driving him crazy.

Mrs. Jones will be, perhaps, between twenty-eight and forty-two years of age, and her problem will be *extremely* familiar to me. Though the details will vary, the frustration she communicates on that afternoon will conform to a well-worn pattern. It will sound something like this.

"John and I were deeply in love when we got married. We struggled during the first two or three years, especially with financial problems, but I knew he loved me and he knew I loved him. But then, something began to change. I'm not sure how to describe it. He received a promotion about five years ago, and that required him to work longer hours. We needed the money, so we didn't mind the extra time he was putting in. But it never stopped. Now he comes home late every evening. He's so tired I can actually hear his feet dragging as he approaches the porch. I look forward to his coming home all day 'cause I have so much to tell him, but he doesn't feel much like talking. So I fix his dinner and he eats it alone. (I usually eat with the kids earlier in the evening.) After dinner, John makes a few phone calls and works at his desk. Frankly, I like for him to talk on the telephone just so I can hear his voice. Then he watches television for a couple of hours and goes to bed. Except on Tuesday night he plays basketball and sometimes he has a meeting at the office. Every Saturday morning he plays golf with three of his friends. Then on Sunday we are in church most of the day. Believe me, there are times when we go for a month or two without having a real, in-depth conversation. You know what I mean? And I get so lonely in that house with three kids climbing all over me. There aren't even any women in our neighborhood I can talk to, because most of them have gone back to work. But there are other irritations about John. He rarely takes me out to dinner and he forgot our anniversary last month, and I honestly don't believe he's ever had a romantic thought. He wouldn't know a rose from a carnation, and his Christmas cards are signed, just "John." There's no closeness or warmth between us, yet he wants to have sex with me at the end of the day. There we are, lying in bed, having had no communication between us in weeks. He hasn't tried to be sweet or understanding or tender, yet he expects me to become passionate and responsive to him. I'll tell you, I can't do it. Sure, I go along with my duties as a wife, but I sure don't get anything out of it. And after the two-minute trip is over and John is asleep, I lie there resenting him and feeling like a cheap prostitute. Can you believe that? I feel *used* for having sex with my own husband! Boy, does that depress me! In fact, I've been awfully depressed lately. My self-esteem is rock bottom right now. I feel like nobody loves me . . . I'm a lousy mother and a terrible wife. Sometimes I think that God probably doesn't love me, either. Well, now I'd better tell you what's been going on between John and me more recently. We've been arguing a lot. I mean *really* fighting. It's the only way I can get his attention, I guess. We had an incredible battle last week in front of the kids. It was awful. Tears. Screaming. Insults. Everything. I spent two nights at my mother's house. Now, all I can think about is getting a divorce so I can escape. John doesn't love me anyway, so what difference would it make? I guess that's why I came to see you. I want to know if I'll be doing the right thing to call it quits."

Mrs. Jones speaks as though she were the only woman in the world who has ever experienced this pattern of needs. But she is not alone. It is my guess that 90 percent of the divorces that occur each year involve at least some of the elements she described—an extremely busy husband who is in love with his work and who tends to be somewhat insensitive, unromantic, and noncommunicative, married to a lonely, vulnerable, romantic woman who has severe doubts about her worth as a human being. They become a matched team: he works like a horse and she nags.

In the hopes of making husbands aware of the universality of their wives' complaints, let me illustrate the point further, only this time, we'll deal with real people instead of a fictitious prototype. Reproduced below is an actual letter (modified to protect the identity of the writer) which represents a thousand others I've received.

Dear Dr. Dobson:

I have read your book *What Wives Wish Their Husbands Knew About Women*. It hit right where I live. Especially the part about low self-esteem. In today's world where so many women have jobs, it is sometimes hard to feel you are worth much if you aren't employed. I mean, some people look down upon a mother like myself who devotes full time to her children and family. But I know Christ doesn't see it that way, and that's what counts.

Unfortunately, I couldn't get my husband to read your book, which brings me to my problem. It is really hard to communicate with my husband when I have to compete with television, kids and work. At mealtimes, which should be a time for talking, he has to listen to Paul Harvey news on the radio. He's not home for the evening meal because he works the 3 to 11 p.m. shift. I really would like him to listen to your "Focus on the Family" program, but he won't.

I'm not permitted to go to Bible Study now (I attended for one year) because he says the kids will pick up diseases from the other children. Of course, I know that's not the real reason. I have a 2½-year-old son and a 3-month-old baby and feel I need to get out among adults. Oh well, I guess I'll keep on praying.

Keep broadcasting your good shows. It would be nice for you to devote another program to husband-wife relationships, mainly communication. Thank you for listening to me.

Sincerely,

Another woman handed me the following note after hearing me speak. It says in a few words what others conveyed with many.

Will you *please* discuss this. Dad arrives home, reads the newspaper, eats dinner, talks on the phone, watches T.V., takes a shower and goes to bed. This is a *constant daily routine*. It never changes. On Sunday we go to church, then come home. We take a nap and then it's back to work again on Monday morning. Our daughter is nine, and we are not communicating, and life is speeding by in this monotonous routine.

I can hear masculine readers saying, "If women want a slower lifestyle, less materialism, and more romantic activities with their husbands, why don't they just tell them so?" They *do* tell them so, in fact. But men find it very difficult to "hear" this message, for some reason.

I'm reminded of the night my father was preaching in an open tent service which was attended by more cats and dogs than people. During the course of his sermon, one large alley cat decided to take a nap on the platform. Inevitably, my father took a step backward and planted his heel squarely on the tail of the tom. The cat literally went crazy, scratching and clawing to free his tail from my father's 6-foot 3-inch frame. But Dad could become very preoccupied while preaching, and he didn't notice the disturbance. There at his feet was a panicky animal, digging holes in the carpet and screaming for mercy, yet the heel did not move. Dad later said he thought the screech came from the brakes of automobiles at a nearby corner. When my father finally walked off the cat's tail, still unaware of the commotion, the tom took off like a Saturn rocket.

This story typifies many twentieth century marriages. The wife is screaming and clawing the air and writhing in pain, but the husband is oblivious to her panic. He is preoccupied with his own thoughts, not realizing that a single step to the right or left could alleviate the crisis. I never cease to be amazed at just how deaf a man can become under these circumstances.

I know of a gynecologist who is not only deaf, but blind as well. He telephoned a friend of mine who is also a physician in the practice of obstetrics and gynecology. He asked for a favor.

"My wife has been having some abdominal problems and she's in particular discomfort this afternoon," he said. "I don't want to treat my own wife and wonder if you'd see her for me?"

My friend invited the doctor to bring his wife for an examination, whereupon he discovered (are you ready for this?) that she was five months pregnant! Her obstetrician husband was so busy caring for other patients that he hadn't even noticed his wife's burgeoning pregnancy. I must admit wondering how in the world this woman ever got his attention long enough to conceive!

A popular western song of a few years back gave expression to these frustrations in male-female relationships. It was entitled "Put Another Log On The Fire," and aimed its salvo at the belly of male chauvinists. The lyrics follow:*

Put another log on the fire
Cook me up some bacon and some beans
And go out to the car and change the tire
Wash my socks and sew my old blue jeans

Come on, Baby

You can fill my pipe and then go fetch my slippers
And boil me up another pot of tea
Then put another log on the fire, Babe
And come and tell me why you're leavin' me.

Now, don't I let you wash the car on Sunday?
Don't I warn you when you're getting fat?
Ain't I a gonna take you fishin' someday?
Well, a man can't love a woman more than that.

Ain't I always nice to your kid sister?
Don't I take her drivin' every night?
So, sit here at my feet
'Cause I like you when you're sweet
And you know it ain't feminine to fight.

Come on, Baby.

You can fill my pipe
And then go fetch my slippers
And boil me up another pot of tea
Then put another log on the fire, Babe
And come and tell me why you're leavin' me.

There's another aspect of the male-female relationship that should also be discussed for the man who wants to understand his wife. Appreciation is expressed to the well-known author Dr. Dennis Guernsey for calling to my attention the research by Rollins and Cannon* and others which reveals a contrasting pattern of "personal satisfaction" by husbands and wives. A woman's satisfaction with her home (which represents the primary job for a homemaker) is never higher than at the time she gets married. But alas, her attitude is destined to slide. It typically deteriorates with the birth of her first baby and continues to sink through the child-rearing years. It reaches a low point in conjunction with the empty-nest syndrome—when the kids leave home. Her satisfaction then rebounds considerably and remains stable during the retirement years.

The husband's job satisfaction follows an opposite pattern. His low point occurs during the early years of marriage, when he accepts a poorly compensated, non-status position. But as he works his way up the ladder, he draws greater emotional rewards (and more money) from his work. This increasing job satisfaction may continue for twenty years or longer, with his work encompassing ever more of his time and energy.

The chart on page 99 will illustrate this contrasting job satisfaction by men and women. Obviously the point of greatest danger occurs in the late thirties and forties, when the wife is most dissatisfied with her assignment and the husband is most enthralled with his. That combination is built for trouble, especially if the man feels no responsibility to help meet his wife's needs and longings. (Please remember that these studies merely reflect *trends* and statistical possibilities. Individuals may respond very differently.)

In the absence of strong and loving support from husbands,

---

*Boyd C. Rollins and Kenneth L. Cannon, *Journal of Marriage and the Family*, May, 1974, p. 271.

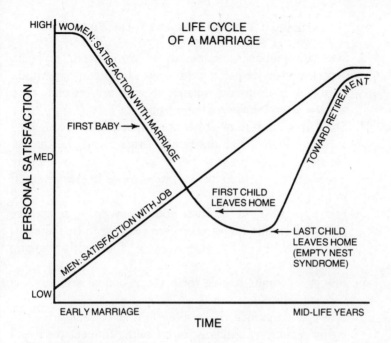

LIFE CYCLE
OF A MARRIAGE

WOMEN: SATISFACTION WITH MARRIAGE

FIRST BABY →

MEN: SATISFACTION WITH JOB

FIRST CHILD
LEAVES HOME

← LAST CHILD
LEAVES HOME
(EMPTY NEST
SYNDROME)

TOWARD RETIREMENT

HIGH

MED

LOW

PERSONAL SATISFACTION

EARLY MARRIAGE

MID-LIFE YEARS

TIME

how do women cope with the circumstances I've described? We all know that behavior does not occur in a vacuum; it is motivated by powerful emotional currents running deep within the personality. Thus, I've observed eight avenues of response that may be taken by a depressed and frustrated wife. They are nonexclusive; in other words, more than one approach can occur simultaneously, or one can lead to others. The eight are as follows:

1. A woman can detach herself from home and family, reinvesting her emotional energy in an outside job. The "back to work" phenomenon by Western women is, in part, a product of this coping mechanism (combined with the pressures of inflation).
2. She can become very angry at men and society for their perceived insults and disrespect. This source of hostility helps to power the women's liberation movement and gives it an aggressive character.

3. She can remain at home in an atmosphere of great depression or despair. Depression is "anger turned inward," and is usually related to low self-esteem. This woman often becomes a classic nagger.

4. She can attempt to meet her pressing needs by getting into an illicit affair. This disastrous avenue usually becomes a dead-end street, leaving her more depressed and lonely than before. We'll discuss its implications in greater detail in chapter 11.

5. She can turn to alcohol and drugs as a temporary palliative. Many homemakers are yielding to this alternative, as evidenced by the rising rate of alcoholism among American women.

6. She can commit suicide (or make a suicidal attempt as a call for help).

7. She can denounce the responsibilities of mothering, by either remaining childless, or by failing to meet the needs of her kids at home. Or she can run away and let Dad take over.

8. The depressed woman can, of course, seek a divorce in the hope of starting afresh with someone more understanding and loving. Today, more than ever, this final alternative looms as *the* accepted method of coping with marital frustration.

None of these coping mechanisms is very productive. In fact, all eight have specific negative consequences. Not even attempted suicide is certain to attract the attention of a mate. I counseled with one woman approximately two weeks after she was released from the hospital. Having made every possible attempt to make contact with her husband, she slid deeper into depression and despair. Finally, she resorted to the ultimate decision. In full view of her husband, she brought all available prescription drugs from the medicine cabinet and proceeded to swallow 206 assorted pills. Her husband stood watching in disbelief. She then went to the bedroom to lie down and die.

But she didn't want to leave this earth, of course. It was a desperate method of dramatizing her condition to the man whose love she needed. Unfortunately, he did not respond. When she realized that he had no intention of rescuing her, she pulled herself together and drove to a nearby hospital. After pumping her stomach, the hospital staff telephoned her husband who came to her bedside. He held her hand for two hours without ever asking why she hadn't wanted to live! In fact, the day he brought her to my office, more than two weeks later, he made his first comment about the event. As he walked around the car to open her door, he said, "I want you to know that you nearly scared me to death a couple of weeks ago!"

Readers might find it difficult to believe that this man loved his wife, but it's true. His lack of attention to her needs was related to a potential business failure that made it difficult for him to "give" to his wife—or even hear her cries. He was facing a crisis of his own, which often occurs in disintegrating marriages.

If the usual coping mechanisms fail to deliver viable solutions to the problems of marital conflict, what *is* the answer? That brings us back to the promise, made in the beginning of this chapter, that I would offer some *straight talk* to husbands and wives. Never before have I abandoned diplomacy in dealing with family issues, but I beg your tolerance in this instance. The current crisis in marriage demands a bold approach that is equal to the magnitude of the danger. You can't kill a dragon with a pop-gun, as they say. Therefore, I'll first take a few shots at men and then turn my guns on the ladies.

A message to the husbands of Christian homemakers:

It is *high* time you realized that your wives are under attack today! Everything they have been taught from earliest childhood is being subjected to ridicule and scorn. Hardly a day passes when the traditional values of the Judeo-Christian heritage are not blatantly mocked and undermined.

—The notion that motherhood is a worthwhile investment of a woman's time suffers unrelenting bombardment.

—And the idea that wives should yield to the leadership of their husbands, as commanded in Ephesians 5:21–33 is considered almost medieval in its stupidity.

—And the concept that a man and woman should become one flesh, finding their identity in each other rather than as separate and competing individuals, is said to be intolerably insulting to women.

—And the belief that divorce is an unacceptable alternative has been abandoned by practically everybody. (Have you heard about Sue and Bob?)

—And the description of the ideal wife and mother, as offered in Proverbs 31:10–31 is now unthinkable for the modern woman. (She's come a long way, baby.)

—And the role of the female as help-meet, bread-baker, wound-patcher, love giver, home builder, and child-bearer is nothing short of disgusting.

All of these deeply ingrained values, which many of your wives are trying desperately to sustain, are continually exposed to the wrath of hell itself. The Western media—radio, television and the press—are working relentlessly to shred the last vestiges of Christian tradition. And your wives who believe in that spiritual heritage are virtually hanging by their thumbs! They are made to feel stupid and old-fashioned and unfulfilled, and in many cases, their self-esteem is suffering irreparable damage. They are fighting a sweeping social movement with very little support from anyone.

Let me say it more directly. For the man who appreciates the willingness of his wife to stand against the tide of public opinion—staying at home in her empty neighborhood in the exclusive company of jelly-faced toddlers and strong willed adolescents—it is about time you gave her some help. I'm not merely suggesting that you wash the dishes or sweep the floor. I'm referring to the provision of emotional support . . . of conversation . . . of making her feel like a lady . . . of building her ego . . . of giving her one day of recreation each week . . . of taking her out to dinner . . . of telling her that you love her. Without these armaments, she is left defenseless against the foes of the family—the foes of *your* family!

But to be honest, many of you husbands and fathers have been thinking about something else. Your wives have been busy attending seminars and reading family literature and studying the Bible, but they can't even get you to enter a discussion about what they've learned. You've been intoxicated with your work and the ego support it provides.

What better illustration can I give than the letter quoted on page 94. It came from a desperate woman whose husband is rarely at home, and even when he's there he has nothing to say. He prefers the company of Paul Harvey, who asks no questions and expects no answers. Furthermore, he's a first-class "punkin eater." You know the story.

> Peter, Peter, Punkin Eater
> Had a wife and couldn't keep her
> Put her in a punkin shell
> And there he kept her very well. . . .

Yeah, Old Pete has got his little woman right where he wants her. She's cooped up in a house with two children under three years of age, changing diapers and wiping noses and cooking meals for him and Mr. Harvey. That's some existence for a living, breathing female with deep needs to be loved and respected. Not only does Peter not intend to meet those needs, but he forbids her to take them elsewhere. He doesn't even want her to go to a Bible study class because, would you believe, he fears his kids will catch a disease. Never mind the disease that is choking the life out of his wife—the disease called *loneliness.* To the wives of all the world's punkin eaters, I say, "Go to the Bible study class anyway!" Submission to masculine leadership does not extend, in my opinion, to behaviors that will be unhealthy for the husband, the wife, and the marriage. Nor should a woman tolerate child abuse, child molestation, or wife-beating.

The message could not be more simple or direct to a Christian man: the Lord has commanded you to "love your wives, even as Christ loved the church, giving His life for it." She needs you now. Will you fit her into your plans?

A message to the wives of busy and unresponsive men:
There are two sides to every coin, and it's time now that we flipped this one over. This chapter has been dominated by the feminine perspective, not because that point of view is more valid or significant, but because it is so poorly understood by the majority of men. I wrote an entire book entitled *What Wives Wish Their Husbands Knew About Women,* for the purpose of conveying some of those frustrations to men. Nevertheless, husbands have their own legitimate complaints to make, too. So brace yourselves, ladies. I'm coming your way.

My strongest words are addressed to the wife of a good man, whom we will call Fred. He loves Barbara and the kids. Honest! He would literally lay down his life for them if required. He doesn't drink. He has never smoked. He has no compulsion to gamble. He wouldn't touch another woman under any imaginable circumstances. He gets up every morning and plods off to work, perhaps holding down a boring, menial job for forty-five years. He brings his salary home and does his best to stretch it through the month. He lives by a moral code that is remarkable for this dishonest era. His income tax return is scrupulously accurate, and he's never stolen so much as a paper clip from his boss. He doesn't beat the kids or kick the dog or flirt with the widow next door. He is as predictable as the sunrise, and I'm sure that God has a special place for him on the other side.

But Steady Freddie has a serious flaw. He was raised in a day when little boys were taught to withhold their thoughts and feelings. "Children are to be seen and not heard," said his parents. He can't remember being hugged or praised, and everybody knows that boys don't cry. So Fred learned his lessons well. He became tough as nails and as silent as the night, but in so doing, he lost touch with his emotions. Now, he *cannot* be spontaneous and affectionate, no matter how hard he tries. It just isn't within him. And most of his thoughts remain unspoken and private.

One would hope that Barbara would accept Fred as he is, since she knew his nature before they were married. In fact, it was his quiet reserve that made Fred attractive to her when they were courting. He always seemed so strong, so in control, compared to her impulsive flightiness. But now Barbara is fed up with her unromantic husband. She is deeply angry because he won't communicate with her, and she nags him incessantly about his alleged "failures" as a husband. He can do *nothing* right and she makes them both miserable year after year.

Let's bring the illustration closer to home. Fred and Boiling Barbara do not represent an unusual combination of personality characteristics. I have seen hundreds of husbands and wives who share their conflict. Many men—not just those who were taught to be inexpressive—find it difficult to match the emotions of their wives. They *cannot* be what their women want them to be. But instead of looking at the *whole* man, assessing his many good qualities as they counterbalance this "flaw," the wife concentrates on the missing element and permits it to dominate their relationship. She's married to a good man . . . but he's not good enough!

Only men who are married to such women fully understand just how wretched life can be. King Solomon had at least one malcontent in his harem, for he wrote "It is better to dwell in the wilderness, than with a contentious and an angry woman" (Prov. 21:19, KJV). He later referred to her dissatisfaction as resembling "a continual dropping in a very rainy day" (Prov. 27:15, KJV). He is right! An agitated woman rants and raves and cries and complains. Her depression is perpetual, destroying vacations, holidays, and the months in between. She may, in retaliation, refuse to cook or clean or take care of the kids. The husband then has the great thrill of coming home to a shattered house and a bitterly angry woman five days a week. And the sad part of the story is that he is often *unable* to become what she wants him to be. He has seriously attempted to rearrange his basic nature on five or six occasions, but to no avail. A leopard can't change its spots, and an unromantic, noncommunicative man simply cannot become a sensitive talker. The marital impasse is set in concrete.

Churning in the mind of the depressed wife is the possibility of divorce. Day and night she contemplates this alternative, weighing the many disadvantages against the one major attraction: *escape*. She worries about the effect of divorce on the kids and wonders how she'll be able to support them and wishes she didn't have to tell her parents. Round and round go the positives and negatives. Should I or shouldn't I? She is both attracted and repelled by the idea of a dissolution.

This contemplative stage reminds me of a classic documentary film which was shot during the earliest days of motion pictures. The cameraman captured a dramatic event that took place on the Eiffel Tower. There, near the top, was a naïve "inventor" who had constructed a set of birdlike wings. He had strapped them to his arms for the purpose of using them to fly, but he wasn't totally convinced that they would work. The film shows him going to the rail and looking downward, then pacing back and forth. Next he stood on the rail trying to get enough courage to jump, then returned to the platform. Even with the primitive camera of those days, the film has captured the internal struggle of that would-be-flier. "Should I or shouldn't I? If the wings work, I'll be famous. If they fail, I'll fall to my death." What a gamble!

The man finally climbed on the rail, turned loose of the nearby beam, and weaved back and forth for a breathless moment of destiny. Then he jumped. The last scene was shot with the camera pointed straight downward, as the man fell like a rock. He didn't even bother to flap his wings on his way to the ground.

In some respects, the depressed homemaker is like the man on the ledge. She knows that divorce is a dangerous and unpredictable leap, but perhaps she will soar with the freedom of a bird. Does she have the courage to jump? No, she'd better stay on the safety of the platform. On the other hand, this could be the long-sought escape. After all, everyone else is doing it. She wavers back and forth in confusion . . . and often takes the plunge.

But what happens to her then? It's been my observation that her "wings" do not deliver the promised support. After the wrenching legal maneuvers and custody fight and property settlement, life returns to a monotonous routine. And what a routine. She has to get a job to maintain a home, but her marketable skills are few. She can be a waitress or a receptionist or a sales lady. But by the time she pays a baby sitter (*if* she can find one) there is little money left for luxuries. Her energy level is in even shorter supply. She comes home exhausted to face the pressing needs of her kids, who irritate her. It's a rugged existence.

Then she looks at her ex-husband who is coping much better. He earns more money than she and the absence of kids provides him more freedom. Furthermore (and this is an important point), in our society there is infinitely more status in being a divorced man than a divorced woman. He often finds another lover who is younger and more attractive than his first wife. Jealousy burns within the mind of the divorcee, who is lonely and, not surprisingly, depressed again.

This is no trumped-up story just to discourage divorce. It is a characteristic pattern. I've observed that many women who seek divorce for the same reasons indicated (as opposed to infidelity) will live to regret their decision. Their husbands, whose good qualities eventually come into view, begin to look very attractive again. But these women have stepped off the ledge . . . and they must yield to the forces of nature.

Divorce is *not* the answer to the problem of busy husbands and lonely wives. Just because the secular world has liberalized its attitudes toward the impermanence of marriage, no such revision has occurred in the Biblical standard. Would you like to know *precisely* what God thinks of divorce? He has made His view abundantly clear in Malachi 2:13–17, especially with reference to husbands who seek a new sexual plaything:

> Yet you cover the altar with your tears because the Lord doesn't pay attention to your offerings anymore, and you receive no blessing from him. "Why has God abandoned us?" you cry. I'll tell you why; it is because the Lord has seen your treachery in divorcing your wives who have been faithful to you through the years, the companions you promised to care for and keep. You were united to your wife by the Lord. In God's wise plan, when you married, the two of you became one person in his sight. And what does he want? Godly children from your union. Therefore guard your passions! Keep faith with the wife of your youth. For the Lord, the God of Israel, says he hates divorce and cruel men. Therefore control your passions—let there be no divorcing of your wives. You have wearied the Lord with your words. "Wearied him?" you ask in fake surprise. "How have we wearied him?" By saying that evil is good, that it pleases the Lord! Or by saying that God won't punish us—he doesn't care (TLB).

If divorce is not the solution, then what can be said on behalf of the emotionally starved woman? First, it will be helpful for her to recognize the *true* source of her frustration. Granted, her husband is not meeting her needs, but I doubt if men have ever responded as women preferred. Did the farmer of a hundred years ago come in from the fields and say, "Tell me how it went with the kids today"? No, he was as oblivious to his wife's nature as Fred is of Barbara's. Then why did the farmer's wife survive while Barbara is climbing the walls? The difference between them can be seen in the *breakdown in the relationship between women!* A century ago, women cooked together, canned together, washed clothes at the creek together, prayed together, went through menopause together, and grew old together. And when a baby was born, aunts and grandmothers and neighbors were there to show the new mother how to diaper and feed and discipline. Great emotional support was provided in this feminine contact. A woman was never really alone.

Alas, the situation is very different today. The extended family has disappeared, depriving the wife of that source of security and fellowship. Her mother lives in New Jersey and her sister is in Texas. Furthermore, American families move every three or four years, preventing any long-term friendships from developing among neighbors. And there's another factor that is seldom admitted: American women tend to be economically competitive and suspicious of one another. Many would not even consider inviting a group of friends to the house until it was repainted, refurnished, or redecorated. As someone said, "We're working so hard to have beautiful homes and there's nobody in them!" The result is isolation—or should I say insulation—and its first cousin: loneliness.

Depriving a woman of all meaningful emotional support from outside the home puts enormous pressure on the husband-wife relationship. The man then becomes her primary source of conversation, ventilation, fellowship, and love. But she's not his only responsibility. He is faced with great pressure, both internal and external, in his job. His self-esteem hangs on the way he handles his business, and the status of the entire family depends on his success. By the time he gets home at night, he has little left with which to prop up his lonely wife . . . even if he understands her.

Let me speak plainly to the wife of the busy but noncommunicative husband: *you cannot depend on this man to satisfy all your needs.* You will be continually frustrated by his failure to comply. Instead, you must achieve a network of women friends with whom you can talk, laugh, gripe, dream, and recreate. There are thousands of homemakers around you who have the same needs and experience. They'll be looking for you as you begin your search for them. Get into exercise classes, group hobbies, church activities, Bible studies, bicycle clubs—whatever. But at all costs, resist the temptation to pull into the four walls of a house, sitting on the pity pot and waiting for your man to come home on his white horse.

We must also deal with the matter of how you "see" your husband. A slight revision in your perception can make him appear much more noble. The gifted author (and my friend) Joyce Landorf has explained this perspective better than anyone I've heard. During the early years of her marriage, she found herself angry at her husband for some of the reasons I've described. Dick inadvertently conveyed insults to her by his manner and personality. For example, just before retiring each evening, he would ask, "Joyce, did you lock the back door?" She always answered affirmatively, whereupon Dick walked to the door to verify that it was bolted. There were only two ways for Joyce to interpret his behavior. Either he thought she was lying about the door, or else he didn't think she had the brains to remember locking it. Both alternatives made her furious. This scenario symbolized a dozen other sources of conflict between them.

Then one night as Dick proceeded to check the lock, the Lord spoke to Joyce.

"Take a good look at him, Joyce," He said.

"What do you mean, Lord?" she replied.

"I have made your husband a door checker. He's a detail man. That's why he's such a good banker. He can examine a list of figures and instantly locate an error that others have overlooked. I gave him that ability to handle banking responsibilities. Yes, Joyce, I made Dick a 'door checker,' and I want you to *accept* him that way."

What a fantastic insight. Many times a man's most irritating characteristic is a by-product of the quality his wife most respects. Perhaps his frugality and stinginess, which she hates, have made him successful in business, which she greatly admires. Or perhaps his attentiveness to his mother's needs, which his wife resents, is another dimension of his devotion to his own family. Or in Fred's case, his cool stability in the face of crisis, which drew Barbara to him, is related to his lack of spontaneity and exuberance during their tranquil days. The point is, *God gave your husband the temperament he wears, and you must accept those characteristics that he cannot change. After all, he must do the same for you.* "For I have learned, in whatsoever state I am, therewith to be content. I know both how to be abased, and I know how to abound: every where and in all things I am instructed both to be full and to be hungry, both to abound and to suffer need. I can do all things through Christ which strengtheneth me" (Phil. 4:11–13, KJV).

Conclusion

There is nothing so ugly as a husband or wife who bitterly attacks and demeans his mate. But nothing is so beautiful as a loving relationship that conforms to God's magnificent design. We'll conclude with a brilliant example of this divinely inspired love. It was written by the surgeon who experienced it. Perhaps you will be deeply moved by his words, as was I.

I stand by the bed where a young woman lies, her face postoperative, her mouth twisted in palsy, clownish. A tiny twig of the facial nerve, the one to the muscles of her mouth, has been severed. She will be thus from now on. The surgeon had followed with religious fervor the curve of her flesh; I promise you that. Nevertheless, to remove the tumor in her cheek, I had cut the little nerve.

Her young husband is in the room. He stands on the opposite side of the bed, and together they seem to dwell in the evening lamplight, isolated from me, private. Who are they, I ask myself, he and this wry-mouth I have made, who gaze at and touch each other so generously, greedily? The young woman speaks.

"Will my mouth always be like this?" she asks.

"Yes," I say, "it will. It is because the nerve was cut."

She nods, and is silent. But the young man smiles.

"I like it," he says. "It is kind of cute."

All at once I *know* who he is. I understand, and I lower my gaze. One is not bold in an encounter with a god. Unmindful, he bends to kiss her crooked mouth, and I so close I can see how he twists his own lips to accommodate to hers, to show her that their kiss still works. I remember that the gods appeared in ancient Greece as mortals, and I hold my breath and let the wonder in. *

---

* Richard Selzer, M.D., *Mortal Lessons: Notes in the Art of Surgery* (New York: Simon & Schuster, 1976), pp. 45–46.

Chapter 9

A Man and the Straight Life

I RECEIVED A CLASSIC letter recently from a woman who described an event that occurred during her first year of marriage. She and her husband became aware that a mouse was cohabiting their apartment—a concept which the woman found intolerable. Her husband set a trap to catch the furry little rodent, and soon did so. However, the type of cage that he constructed permitted them to capture the creature alive, presenting the question, "What do we do with him now?" Neither husband nor wife had the courage to murder the mouse in cold blood, but they didn't want to let him go, either. They finally settled on a solution. They would drown him.

The husband filled a bucket with water and carefully placed the cage, mouse included, into the liquid. The couple then left home for two hours, so as not to witness the final struggle. But when they returned, they found that the water didn't quite cover the top of the cage. The mouse had made the same discovery, and managed to keep the tip of his nose above the surface by standing on one toe.

I never learned how the final execution was administered. You see, the wife told me the story not to acquaint me with the plight of her mouse, but to illustrate her *own* difficulties. She said that the rodent, standing on one aching toe, came to symbolize her first year of marriage. She survived, but only by stretching to keep her nose above water.

Alas, the illustration applies to millions of other husbands and wives as well. Only by stress and strain are they able to avoid drowning in a sea of never-ending responsibilities. I want to devote the remainder of this chapter to such people, who are coping with the pressures of the "straight life." Let me begin by defining my terms.

The straight life for a homemaker is washing dishes three hours a day; it is cleaning sinks and scouring toilets and waxing floors; it is chasing toddlers and mediating fights between preschool siblings. (One mother said she had raised three "tricycle motors," and they had worn her out.) The straight life is driving your station wagon to school and back twenty-three times per week; it is grocery shopping and baking cupcakes for the class Halloween party. The straight life eventually means becoming the parent of an ungrateful teenager, which I assure you is no job for sissies. (It's difficult to let your adolescent find himself—especially when you know he isn't even looking!) Certainly, the straight life for the homemaker can be an exhausting experience, at times.

The straight life for a working man is not much simpler. It is pulling your tired frame out of bed, five days a week, fifty weeks out of the year. It is earning a two-week vacation in August, and choosing a trip that will please the kids. The straight life is spending your money wisely when you'd rather indulge in a new whatever; it is taking your son bike riding on Saturday when you want so badly to watch the baseball game; it is cleaning out the garage on your day off after working sixty hours the prior week. The straight life is coping with head colds and engine tune-ups and crab grass and income-tax forms; it is taking your family to church on Sunday when you've heard every idea the minister has to offer; it is giving a portion of your income to God's work when you already wonder how ends will meet. The straight life for the ordinary, garden-variety husband and father is everything I have listed and more . . . much more.

Consider, now, the straight life for those who carry an especially heavy burden. I think of all the single parents who deserve our admiration. They must complete the tasks ordinarily assigned to husbands *and* wives, without the support and love of a partner. The straight life for them runs not on level ground but uphill seven days a week. Occasionally I meet a man or woman whose journey seems almost unbearable. I will never forget the telephone conversation I had with a young mother last year. We were broadcasting live on the radio, and I was attempting to answer questions of callers who sought my advice. The program was recorded, permitting me to reflect on that emotional conversation. The soft, feminine voice of a girl, perhaps twenty-three years of age, still echoes in my mind.

She was the mother of two preschool children, the youngest being a thirteen-month-old with cerebral palsy. He could neither talk nor walk nor respond in the manner of other children his age. The older brother, then three years of age, apparently resented the attention given the baby, and constantly tested the limits of his mother's authority. As we conversed, however, I learned of additional difficulties. Her husband had been unable to withstand these pressures and had departed a few months earlier. So there was this young woman, burdened by the guilt and trials of a sick baby and a rebellious toddler, also confronted by abandonment and rejection from her husband. My heart ached for her.

After broadcasting this conversation, we received dozens of

letters from listeners who requested the mother's name and address. People wanted to pray for her and offer financial aid. But I couldn't help them. I only knew her as a voice—a voice which conveyed sadness and pain and fear and courage and faith. Obviously, this young woman walks the straight life day by day . . . alone.

My point is that the straight life eventually gets heavy . . . for all of us who are walking that line. There are times when we ask, "What am I doing here? Is this all there is to life? Am I destined to plod through my remaining years with this never-ending responsibility?"

Until thirty years ago, only one socially acceptable answer was offered in response to those weary questions: "Keep plugging! You have mouths to feed, backs to clothe, a boss to please, and a home to maintain. Clench your fists, and get back to work." It may not have been a comforting conclusion, but it produced *stability* in families and in society.

Today, a new answer is being offered. It says, "I wouldn't take it any more. You're a dope for being everybody's grubby slave. Why don't you chuck it all and start a new life? The kids will adjust, somehow. They don't appreciate you anyway. Maybe you can find a new lover, someone who really cares. C'mon, baby. Grab all the gusto you can get, 'cause you'll only go around once in life!"

What I'm saying is that for all of us who walk the straight life today, there are *voices* that continually invite us to leave it. Examine any magazine or turn on the television set and you're likely to encounter these opponents of self-discipline and responsibility. Let's examine four of the voices that are most influential in encouraging people to abandon the straight life.

The first is the voice of *pleasure*. To the person who has worked seventy hours a week for a period of years, the possibility of enjoyment can become a major attraction. I consulted with one man who left his wife and married his secretary. I asked him what motivated this dramatic decision, and he answered immediately.

"I am the father of four kids," he said. "I have been a full-time husband and father for ten years, putting up with constant noise and bickering and financial pressures at home. I have rarely had any time to myself, and my life has been one long obligation. Then Martha came onto the scene, and I went with her, because, quite frankly, fun and games looked good to me."

This man was obviously "pulled" off the straight life by the voice of pleasure.

The second voice that influences more women than men can be called the *lure of romanticism*. Wives, especially those married to busy husbands, crave the excitement of romantic encounters. They long for "Some enchanted evening, across a crowded room"! Another song that gives expression to these needs is entitled "The Dreams of the Everyday Housewife." Its lyrics describe a lonely woman in a tattered housedress, thumbing through the pages of an old scrapbook. She finds a crushed and dried flower, given to her so long ago on the night of the high school prom. She was so charming that evening, and the boys were stunned by her beauty. Then just for a moment, her housedress becomes an evening gown, and she twirls before the mirror in ecstasy. She is beautiful again and the object of desire and envy. But it is just a passing fantasy, and the vision fades. Now she hungers for a small measure of that romantic excitement in her life. She is not alone. This craving for a Cinderella-type encounter is a very common yearning among wives and mothers. That is why the *lure of romanticism* entices so many women off the straight life.

The third voice calling adults off the path of responsibility is the *desire for extramarital sexual relations*. Dr. Robert Whitehurst, from the Department of Sociology at the University of Windsor, Ontario, was once asked this question: "Do most men, at some point, have extramarital desires?" His reply, published in the journal *Sexual Behavior* included these comments: " . . . *All* men from the first day of marriage onward *think* about this possibility. . . ." " . . . *Although* these tendencies toward extramarital sexual activity diminish in later middle age and beyond, they never entirely vanish or disappear in normal men."

These strong statements leave little room for exceptions, but I'm inclined to agree with their conclusions. The lure of infidelity has incredible power to influence human behavior. Even Christian men, who are committed to God and their wives, must deal with the same sexual temptations. Nevertheless, the Apostle Peter wrote in unmistakable terms about people who yield to these pressures: "With eyes full of adultery, they never stop sinning; they seduce the unstable; they are experts in greed—an accursed brood! *They have left the straight way* and wandered off to follow the way of Balaam son of Beor, who loved the wages of wickedness" (2 Pet. 2:14–15, NIV, emphasis added).

That brings us to the fourth voice, which is even more influential than those considered to this point. I've called it *ego needs*. Both men and women appear equally vulnerable to this powerful desire to be admired and respected by members of the opposite sex. Therefore, those who become entangled in an affair often do so because they want to prove that they are still attractive to women (or men). The thrill comes from knowing "someone finds me sexy, or intelligent, or pretty or handsome. That person enjoys hearing me talk . . . likes the way I think . . . finds me exciting." These feelings emanate from the core of the personality—the ego—and they can make a sane man or woman behave in foolish and dishonorable ways.

I'm reminded of the seventh chapter of Proverbs, wherein King Solomon is warning young men not to patronize prostitutes. These are the words of Israel's wisest king:

> I was looking out the window of my house one day, and saw a simple-minded lad, a young man lacking common sense, walking at twilight down the street to the house of this wayward girl, a prostitute. She approached him, saucy and pert, and dressed seductively. She was the brash, coarse type, seen often in the streets and markets, soliciting at every corner for men to be her lovers.

She put her arms around him and kissed him, and with a saucy look she said, "I've decided to forget our quarrel! I was just coming to look for you and here you are! My bed is spread with lovely, colored sheets of finest linen imported from Egypt, perfumed with myrrh, aloes and cinnamon. Come on, let's take our fill of love until morning, for my husband is away on a long trip. He has taken a wallet full of money with him, and won't return for several days."

So she seduced him with her pretty speech, her coaxing and her wheedling, until he yielded to her. *He couldn't resist her flattery.* He followed her as an ox going to the butcher, or as a stag that is trapped, waiting to be killed with an arrow through its heart. He was as a bird flying into a snare, not knowing the fate awaiting it there.

Listen to me, young men, and not only listen but obey; don't let your desires get out of hand; don't let yourself think about her. Don't go near her; stay away from where she walks, lest she tempt you and seduce you. For she has been the ruin of multitudes—a vast host of men have been her victims. If you want to find the road to hell, look for her house (Prov. 7:6–27, TLB, emphasis added).

Notice that Solomon did not say that the young man could not withstand the sexual enticement of this woman. It was her *flattery* that he found irresistible. She made him think she admired him, and that was the fatal blow. I only wish Solomon had acknowledged that millions of *women* have been caught in the same snare, set by sweet-talking men. Both males and females are equally vulnerable to ego needs and flattery.

Let me diagram this path of responsibility and the voices that call to us from the world of folly.

PLEASURE   ROMANTICISM

———————————————————————————————————
                STRAIGHT LIFE

        SEX   EGO NEEDS

I've found it interesting to observe men and women who decide to leave the straight life in pursuit of alien voices. Rarely do they make a sudden left or right turn and plunge into an affair or a differing lifestyle. Instead, they make very small, safe departures from that line, and then return for a time of evaluation. (See diagram.)

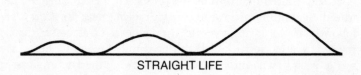

STRAIGHT LIFE

In the early stages, an observer might not even recognize the behavior as an illicit response. It may represent a luncheon with a secretary that lasts only thirty minutes longer than usual. Both the man and woman could justify their actions, if pressed. They were talking about business most of the time. But both of them know that their business conversation is not responsible for the excitement they feel inside. They are flirting with a departure from the straight life. Later in the day she hands him a sheet of paper, and as he accepts it, he allows his hand to pass gently over hers. It's no big deal. They have done nothing wrong. But both of them are making tiny "blips" off the path of responsibility. If they don't check their inclinations at that point, the blip will become a bulge, and the illicit relationship will grow. Such matters are almost always progressive unless deliberately quenched. Finally, the love affair that began with a long lunch becomes a flaming passion that is incompatible with the straight life. Then the break occurs dramatically.

Perhaps it *appears* that Tom or Marge suddenly abandoned their homes, marriages, kids and jobs . . . but you can be sure that they've contemplated and "tested" the break for weeks.

But now we come to a very important question. What happens to the person who chases after the exciting voices? Do

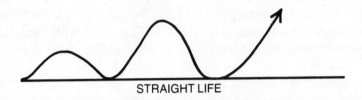

STRAIGHT LIFE

they really live happily ever after? Hardly! I have watched those who departed from the world of responsibility, and an interesting phenomenon invariably occurs: they eventually establish another straight life! The grass is greener on the other side of the fence, but it still has to be mowed. Sooner or later, the pleasure of an illicit affair has to come to an end. Folks have to get back to work. Nor can the fantastic romantic feeling last forever. In fact, the new lover soon becomes rather commonplace, just like the former husband or wife. His or her flaws come into focus, and the couple has their first fight. That takes the edge off the thrill. And the sexual relationship gradually loses its breathtaking quality because it's no longer new. There are times when it doesn't appeal at all. But most significantly, the man and woman eventually turn their thoughts to earning a living and cooking and cleaning and paying taxes again, permitting ego needs to accumulate as before. Alas, after the emotions have been on a moon-shot, they are destined to come back down to earth once more.

Then what does our amorous couple do when they conclude for the second time that the straight life has become intolerably heavy? I am acquainted with men and women, and so are you, who have ripped from one straight life to another in vain search of prolonged pleasure and sex- and ego-gratification. In so doing, they leave in their wake former husbands or wives who feel rejected and bitter and unloved. They produce little children who crave the affection of a father or mother . . . but never find it. All that is left on the march toward old age is a series of broken relationships and shattered lives and hostile children. A scriptural principle foretells the inevitable outcome: "Then when lust hath conceived, it bringeth forth sin; and sin, when it is finished, bringeth forth death" (James 1:15, KJV).

Our humanistic society has considered these painful consequences of divorce, and has offered various "solutions" to troubled families. One of those suggestions, which must rank as the most ridiculous idea in the history of marriage, is that we should bring infidelity *into* the straight life. This concept of non-exclusive marriage was described by Nina and George O'Neill, in their best-selling book, *Open Marriage*. They proposed that husbands and wives permit one another to bed down with whomever they pleased, without so much as a tip of the hat to the spouse. Even the O'Neills now admit that their idea didn't work. It seems that they overlooked the presence of jealousy in the relationship. Who would have thought it?

Dick Hobson said it better, writing in the *Los Angeles Magazine*,

> . . . our character structure is built in, and we can't get free that easily. Changing the externals—the social mores—can give the dangerous illusion that something has really changed. So now you're telling us that sex is good and we should have lots of it; then why are we not? Because we're still being run by an internal standard that never heard of the Sexual Revolution (April, 1977, p. 197).

Back to the drawing boards. If we can't bring infidelity into marriage, maybe we can make it easier to escape from the straight life. Toward this end, John F. Whitaker, M.D., has written "A Personal Marriage Contract" which is almost as foolish as *Open Marriage*. It was published in *Woman's Day*, of all places, and bore this headline: "A set of contemporary guidelines for the young couple who are contemplating marriage today." Whitaker then provided a contract to be signed, witnessed, and dated by the parties involved. If you can read the conditions of the contract without becoming indignant, you're made of different stuff than I. Let me quote a few of the items:

> I understand that nothing is forever; that there are no absolute guarantees, and that NOW is the only real forever.

> I cannot make you happy or unhappy, but I can make myself happy. My happiness will be an invitation for you to join me in happiness, joy and love.

> I will set my own standards and ultimately depend upon myself for approval.

> I give up the myth that there is a "one and only" who will make me happy.

> When I make commitments to do what I want to do, then I am being free. . . . There is no freedom without responsibility.

> Since I understand that we cannot be everything to each other, I will respect and value the importance of your having separate play and work activities with separate friends and co-workers.

> I understand that there will be pain as well as joy, and I accept the risk of a brief period when we part. [Notice that the author does not say "if we part."] I know that I must ultimately give up everyone I love unless he dies first.

> I will love, honor, respect (but not obey or subjugate myself to you) until either of us changes his mind and maintains a change of attitude for a period of one year or until the termination date of the contract.

> Don't expect me to accept you as you are when you fail to maintain mental attractiveness and fail to take care of your mind.

Don't expect me to accept you as you are when you fail to maintain physical attractiveness and fail to take care of your body.

I will put myself first. By keeping myself full, satisfied, and not hungry, I will have an abundance of joy, love, and caring to give you.

I will own my separate money and property, and enjoy sharing ownership with you of our common money and property.

Whenever we are confronted with a problem, I will resolve my feelings first, and then, with a cool mind, rationally solve any mutual problems with you.

While I reserve the right to have private areas of my life that I will not share with you, I will not lie to you either by word or action or by failure to share relevant information that affects our relationship.

I will not give come-on signals to others for sexual relations when I see that you feel threatened. I will count on you to recognize, admire and stroke me for my sexuality and attractiveness as a man or woman. *

A place is provided on the contract for the designated term of the agreement. The instructions read, "On the date of termination, we will reconfirm or renegotiate the contract; or we will cease being WITH each other, will part in a friendly manner and will go on with our lives separately."

Isn't that a sweet basis on which to build a marriage? The author is proposing that a straight life be established, but that the newlyweds agree in advance not to stay on it very long. And

---

* From the book *Personal Marriage Contract* by John F. Whitaker, M.D., Copyright 1976, by John F. Whitaker, M.D., published by OK Street, Inc., Dallas, Texas, 1976.

you can be assured that they won't. One basic flaw runs through the easy-out concept: it underestimates the power of sex and marriage to make us "one flesh," and fails to anticipate the ripping and tearing of that flesh at the moment of disintegration. Like *Open Marriage*, it will only bring pain to those who apply its godless philosophy.

Then what *is* the answer to a straight life that oppresses its family members? What solutions are consistent with the Christian faith? The remedy, as I have been attempting to say throughout this book, is to bring those external voices *into* the straight life. You see, the greater the frustration on the path of responsibility, the louder are the voices that call us from it. To lessen their appeal, we must simply meet the same needs within the context of marriage. First, every couple should reserve time specifically for pleasure. Husbands and wives should go on a date at least once a week, leaving children at home. Likewise, some form of sports or recreational activity should be enjoyed as a family, whether it be tennis, golf, swimming, skiing, or some other option.

Second, every husband and wife should seek to keep the romantic fires aglow in the relationship, by the use of love notes and surprises and candlelight dinners and unexpected weekend trips, among other possibilities.

Third, couples *must* reserve some of their time and energy for meaningful sexual activity. Tired bodies make for tired sex. The physical aspect of the relationship can be approached creatively, and indeed, must be.

Fourth, the most successful marriages are those where both husband and wife seek to build the self-esteem of the other. How tragic it is when a destructive relationship prevails. It makes me uncomfortable even to be in the company of a man and woman who are taking verbal swats at each other, attempting to insult and debase the partner. Ego needs *can* be met within the bonds of marriage, and nothing contributes more

125

to closeness and stability than to convey respect for the personhood of the spouse.

But who will invest the necessary effort to bring these amenities into marriage? Again, my observation is that most women are merely waiting for their husbands to assume leadership in this objective. They are more than willing to follow suit, but they can't do the job alone. It's a game only two can play.

SECTION IV

A MAN AND HIS WORK

Chapter 10

A Man and His Work

Having DISCUSSED the straight life in general terms, it is appropriate now that we examine the specific responsibility of a man's work. This topic has great relevance to the central theme of this book, which has focused on a man's priorities and the importance he gives to his family. In twentieth-century America, it is almost inevitable that a vigorous competition arises between a man's job and his home. Achieving a balance between two areas of responsibility requires constant vigilance, and, quite frankly, most men tip the scales dramatically in the direction of their employment.

I have already admitted that I have also struggled to achieve a proper perspective between my profession and my family. Just when I think I have conquered the dragon of overcommitment, I say "yes" a few times when I should have said, "no, thanks," and the monster arises to maul me again. I know of no easier mistake to make, nor one that has such devastating implications for the family.

In chapter 5, I described an extremely hectic period of my life occurring in 1969, and how my father helped me rearrange my priorities for the better. Nevertheless, the *worst* siege of overcommitment I've ever experienced came in the fall of 1977. I went through six weeks of incredible pressure, involving obligations that should have been spread over six months. I still don't know what wave of stupidity caused me to yield to such nonsense. I wasn't forced. No one threatened my life. I was not financially pressed. I can recall having *no* excuse. I simply relaxed my guard for a few weeks and found myself in a race for survival.

I had agreed to speak at various functions around the country on five out of six consecutive weekends. That, in itself, was ridiculous, meaning I would not see my children on a Saturday for more than a month. But at the same time, I was facing deadlines on a new book, three new tape albums, a weekly radio broadcast, and a random IRS audit (lucky me). To compound matters, the San Antonio trip and near death of my dad, mentioned earlier, occurred in the middle of this period. Fatigue mounted week by week as I ran to catch planes and write speeches and search for tax receipts.

The climax occurred in early October when I flew to Cincinnati to participate in a Praise Gathering, sponsored by Mr. Bill Gaither. I lost a night of sleep going in, due to the time change, and then spent two days standing before crowds ranging from two hundred to eight thousand people. It was an exhilarating time of teaching and sharing and counseling, but it squeezed the last drop of energy from my frame. I staggered toward the airport in a state of utter exhaustion. One thought pulsed through my head as the plane headed west: *"It's over!"*

For six weeks I had had no time to myself. My great desire was to crawl through the front door of my house and remain in isolation for at least seven days. Above all, I wanted to watch the USC-Alabama football game on television the next day. That, to me, is therapy at its best (provided USC wins!).

Let's leave that westbound plane for a moment and journey to a home in Arcadia, California, where my wife, Shirley, is also approaching the end of a siege. For six long weeks she has run the home without benefit of a man. It has been her task to discipline and train and guide and feed and medicate and bathe two rambunctious kids. Needless to say, she is *also* nearing the point of exhaustion. Furthermore, Shirley has hardly seen her husband since the first of September, and her emotional needs have been on a prolonged "hold." One thought gives her strength to continue: "At last, Jim is coming home and he'll take over!"

It takes no great analyst to observe that Shirley and I approached that final weekend on a collision course! An explosion was just a matter of time, because each of us was too exhausted to consider the needs of the other.

I should pause to explain the relationship that Shirley and I enjoy as husband and wife. God has blessed our marriage in such a beautiful way. Shirley is, truly, my very best friend on the face of the earth. In fact, if I had one free evening that I could spend with any person of my choice, there is no one in the world who would outrank my own wife. It is amazing that two people could live together for nineteen years and yet find so much to talk about and share day by day. We have also grown in mutual understanding so that it is rarely necessary to quarrel and argue at this stage in our lives. The "power struggle" of earlier years is largely over. Nevertheless, I'm here to tell you that Shirley and I had a dandy fight on the weekend following the Praise Gathering!

I arrived home on Friday night, and Shirley greeted me warmly at the door. We chatted about recent events and the kids and routine matters before sleep overtook us. The next morning went smoothly enough . . . at least until breakfast was over. We ate on the patio in the back yard. But as we were finishing the meal, our attitudinal differences suddenly blew up in our faces.

"Uh, Jim," said Shirley, "as you know, seventy-five members from the Singles Department at our church will be using our house tonight, and I need you to help me get ready for them. First, I want you to wash down the patio umbrella for me."

My blood pressure immediately shot up to about 212, and steam began to curl from my ears. Didn't Shirley know how hard I had worked? What kind of a slave driver is this woman? Doesn't she understand how badly I need this day? Well, I'll tell you something! I'm watching that football game, and if Shirley doesn't like it she can just lump it!

I don't recall what words I used to convey these thoughts, but I must have gotten the idea across. Shirley stood startled for a moment, then went in the house and slammed the door. I sat under the dirty umbrella for a few minutes, filled with righteous indignation. I never felt so justified in my life. "After all, you know, I'm not an iron man. I need rest, too, and I'm gonna have it!"

So I had my way. I watched the USC-Alabama game in my study, but the tension around me was incredible. Silence prevailed between husband and wife. Not a word had been spoken since our terse interchange in the back yard. Then our anger began to turn into mutual hurt, which is even more damaging to communication.

The seventy-five church members came that evening and were served refreshments on the patio. They didn't seem to notice the dirty umbrella. They eventually departed, leaving me in the company of a mute female who still acted like the entire episode was my fault. Isn't that just like a woman?!

Then came the awkward time of day called bedtime. I climbed into my side of the king-sized bed and parked as close to the edge as possible without plunging over the precipice. Shirley did likewise, clinging tenaciously to her "brink." At least eight feet of mattress separated us. No words were spoken. There were, however, frequent sighs from both parties, accompanied by much rolling and tossing. Shirley finally got up to take two aspirin and then returned to bed. Fifteen minutes later I turned on the light to put some nose drops in my nostrils. What followed was one of the worst nights of sleep in my life.

The next morning was Sunday, which presented more uncomfortable moments. We dressed and went to our adult class, still bearing deep wounds and resentment. And wouldn't you know, the teacher chose that morning to talk about marital harmony and God's plan for husbands and wives. Shirley and I nodded and smiled in agreement, but we felt like kicking each other under the table. It made me suspect that many other couples were also putting on a good front to hide their real feelings. (I later told this story to the same class and found that my suspicions were accurate.)

I wish I could say that the problem was resolved on Sunday afternoon, but such was not the case. Nor did it end on Monday or Tuesday. By Wednesday morning, we were sick to death of this silent warfare. We were both more rested by that time, and the issue began to lose some of its fire. I told Shirley I wanted her to join me for breakfast at a restaurant, and announced my intention of going to work late.

What occurred was a beautiful time of communication and love. I began to see that Shirley was in the same state of need that I had been. She began to understand the depths of my fatigue. We talked it out and reestablished the closeness that makes life worth living. Not only did we survive the crisis, but we learned several valuable lessons and grew from the experience.

I have not written the details of this conflict for the purpose of entertaining you. Rather, it is my conviction that *most* couples have fought over the same issue, and the lessons that Shirley and I learned from it can be helpful to others. Three distinct concepts emerged which may assist you in handling a similar episode in your marriage. Let me enumerate them.

1. *All miscommunication results from differing assumptions.*

It is now clear that my battle with Shirley resulted entirely from our differing assumptions about the approaching weekend, and our failure to clarify those attitudes before they collided. I assumed that my responsibilities as husband and father would not resume until I had been given a chance to rest and recuperate. That was a reasonable expectation, but it happened to differ with Shirley's assumption. She felt that her lonely tour of duty at home was to end with my return from the wars, and that I would accept the burden from her weary shoulders with the rise of the Saturday sun. It was a reasonable supposition, but not in harmony with mine. We could have avoided the conflict by a five-minute conversation prior to the umbrella incident.

I should have said, "Shirley, I know you've had it rough here at home these past six weeks, and I intend to help you pull things together. But I'm going to ask you to understand me for a few more days. I'm more tired than I ever remember being, and I find it difficult to even engage in conversation. If you'll let me hole up for a few days . . . watch some football games on television and sleep a lot . . . I'll pick up my domestic responsibilities the first part of next week."

Shirley would have understood this request and honored it. That's the kind of woman she is. Likewise, if she had said to me, "Jim, these past six weeks have been extremely hectic here at home. I know you couldn't help it, but we've missed your presence here. Just as soon as possible, I need you to get involved with the kids, and for that matter, I want to be with you, too. And besides, there's *one* task I can't do that I would appreciate your handling Saturday morning. You see, the umbrella is dirty and—"

The brief explanation would have helped me understand Shirley's situation. But in reality, we allowed our differing assumptions to remain unspoken . . . and you know the rest of the story.

Bad marriages are saturated with differing assumptions between husbands and wives. He assumes that he has met his marital responsibilities by earning a living for the family. She assumes that he should also meet her romantic needs and occasionally help with the kids. Constant friction occurs where those diverse views collide. He assumes that sexual intercourse is his prerogative, whenever and wherever he desires it. She assumes that sexual intercourse is to occur after they've enjoyed a time of communication, love, and mutual respect. Great conflict occurs between those contrasting perspectives. He assumes that their money belongs primarily to him, since he earned it. She assumes that she's entitled to half the resources as the law implies. The list of these commonly differing assumptions is virtually endless, and the havoc they inflict is apparent in every divorce court.

One of the purposes of marriage counseling, at least as I perceive it, is to work through those differing points of view in search of compromise and harmony.

2. *The hostility in many marriages is a direct expression of deep hurt between husband and wife.*

Returning to my conflict with Shirley, remember that neither of us sought to hurt the other person. Our initial anger was not motivated by malice or vindictiveness, but by a sense of having been wronged. That situation often underlies marital conflict. Being wounded in spirit gives birth to anger and resentment, leading to destructive words between husbands and wives.

Let's quietly visit a newlywed couple who are in the midst of a terrible battle. She is screaming insults at him and he hurls the meanest concoctions back at her. They stand red-faced in their apartment, disassembling one another's egos. Observers might be surprised to learn that their *basic* problem is not one of mutual anger. They have both been *hurt* by the behavior of the other. The accusations they sling back and forth are merely reactions to the pain inside. Nevertheless, their words serve to deepen the original wounds and intensify the pain. It becomes a vicious cycle that can quickly destroy a relationship.

That cycle could be broken if *one* of the combatants could muster the courage to talk about his own pain, rather than increasing the discomfort of his partner.

"John, I cooked this delicious meal . . . spent three hours in the kitchen trying to please you. Then you didn't even call to say you'd be late. Frankly, it hurt my feelings and made me feel that you don't respect me."

John can receive that message without having to say hurtful things in response. But if Mary calls him "irresponsible, uncaring, heartless and just like your mother," then the battle lines are drawn. Understanding these dynamics of personal conflict can help lessen the hostility when disagreements occur.

3. *Overcommitment is the Number One Marriage Killer.*

This third lesson growing out of our conflict is the most important, and reiterates a concept presented throughout this book. Not only are fatigue and time pressure destructive to parent-child relationships, but they undermine even the healthiest of marriages. How can a man and woman communicate with each other when they're too worn out even to talk? How can they pray together when every moment is programmed to the limit? How can they enjoy a sexual relationship when they are exhausted at the end of every day? How can they "date" one another or take walks in the rain or sit by a fire when they face the tyranny of an unfinished "to do" list?

From this vantage point, I have to admit that my fight with Shirley was primarily *my* fault. Not that I was wrong in wanting to rest after arriving home. But I was to blame for foolishly overcommitting my time during that period. The conflict would never have occurred if I had not scheduled myself wall to wall for six weeks. My lack of discipline in my work caused Shirley and me to become exhausted, which brought a chain reaction of negative emotions: irritability, self-pity, petulance, selfishness, and withdrawal. Few marriages can survive a long-term dose of that bitter medicine.

I mentioned earlier that I shared this story with my adult Sunday school class a few weeks after it occurred. My comments happened to have been recorded that day, and a cassette tape package is now being marketed under the title *How to Save Your Marriage*. It has produced some interesting correspondence from those who have heard the message. One of those letters is reproduced below with permission from the writer.

Dear Dr. Dobson:

It is one o'clock in the morning—I have just finished listening to your tape "How To Save Your Marriage." In addition to my regular job as treasurer/general manager of a major corporation, I carry an untold number of responsibilities with church, Christian, and community organizations.

I have listened to your tape only one time but am left with a sense of absolute frustration and guilt. I am the prototype of the man you have described so aptly. And, I don't know how to extricate myself from this situation. Practically everything which you point out applies to my case—overscheduling, economic need, etc., etc.

I have three children: second-year college, fourth-year high school, first-year high school—and I know that they will never look back on times with me as the best days of their childhood. This really hurts.

I know that something must be done. I know that the Lord is able. I am not sure that I can change. I guess my purpose in writing this letter—at this hour—is somewhat therapeutic: to acknowledge my condition, to take a concrete first step in that same direction, and to ask your prayers on my behalf.

I have two of your books which I have glanced at or skimmed through. Your taped message, however, was listened to while working. I don't recall ever hearing a more honest and practical message in my twenty years as a Christian.

Thanks for your sharing in such a practical way. My present thought is to let my wife listen to the tape and then let it serve as a basis for an in-depth discussion. It occurs to me that perhaps I should ask the kids to listen, also, and perhaps this can serve as a beginning of new relationships with them. I don't know.

Again, thinking of the "concrete step," I'll mail this letter on the way home.

Thanks for your honesty.

Sincerely in Christ,

I've included this letter to illustrate what men already know: it isn't easy to implement a slower lifestyle. Prior commitments have to be met. Financial pressures must be confronted. The employer seldom *asks* if you want to accept a new assignment. Your business would fail without your supervision. Your patients have no other physician to whom they can turn. Several of your church members are in the hospital and awaiting your ministerial visit. There seems to be no place to stop. Also, we must not overlook that ever-present masculine need to succeed . . . to push . . . to strive . . . to accomplish.

Besides, isn't everyone else doing the same thing? Sure they are. I don't even know any men who aren't running at a breathless pace. My physician, my lawyer, my accountant, my handyman, my mechanic, my pastor, my next-door neighbor. There is symbolic sweat on the brow of virtually every man in America. Most of these husbands and fathers will admit that they're working too hard, but an interesting response occurs when this subject is raised. They have honestly convinced themselves that their overcommitment is a *temporary* problem.

"Well, this is a difficult year, you see, because I'm going to night school and trying to earn a living at the same time. But it won't always be so hectic at our house. I figure I'll have the degree by a year from June. Then pressure will ease up."

or . . . "My wife and I just bought this new business, and it's gonna take us a year to get it rolling. Then we can hire the help we need. Until then, though, we're having to work ten to twelve hours a day. That cuts into our family life quite a bit, but it won't last very long."

or . . . "We just moved into a new house, and I've had to put in all the yards and build on a room in back. Every Saturday and most evenings are invested in that project. My son keeps asking me to fly a kite with him and go fishing and stuff, and I wish I could. I keep telling him if he can wait 'til next summer we'll have a lot of time to do those things."

or . . . "My wife had a baby two weeks ago and he's not sleeping through the night, so our schedule is all haywire now. I figure it'll be kinda difficult until we get him in kindergarten."

Most people can tell you with a straight face that the pressures they feel are the result of temporary circumstances. Their future will be less hectic. A slower day is coming. A light shines at the end of the dark tunnel. Unfortunately, their optimism is usually unjustified. It is my observation that the hoped-for period of tranquility rarely arrives. Instead, these short term pressures have a way of becoming sandwiched back to back, so that families emerge from one crisis and sail directly into another. Thus, we live our entire lives in the fast lane, hurtling down the road toward heart failure. We have deluded ourselves into believing that circumstances have forced us to work too hard for a short time, when, in fact, we are driven from *within*. We lack the discipline to limit our entanglements with the world, choosing instead to be dominated by our work and the materialistic gadgetry it will bring. And what is sacrificed in the process are the loving relationships with wives and children and friends who give life meaning.

Conclusion

I, for one, have examined America's breathless lifestyle and find it to be *unacceptable*. At forty-three years of age (I would be forty-four but I was sick a year), I have been thinking about the stages of my earthly existence and what they will represent at its conclusion. There was a time when all of my friends were graduating from high school. Then I recall so many who entered colleges around the country. And alas, I lived through a phase when everyone seemed to be getting married. Then a few years later, we were besieged by baby shower announcements. You see, my generation is slowly but relentlessly moving through the decades, as have 2400 generations that preceded it. Now, it occurs to me that a time will soon come when my friends will be dying. ("Wasn't it tragic what happened to Charles Painter yesterday?")

My aunt, Naomi Dobson, wrote me shortly before her death in 1978. She said, "It seems like every day another of my close friends either passes away or is afflicted with a terrible disease." Obviously, she was in that final phase of her generation. Now she is also gone.

What does this have to do with my life, today? How does it relate to yours? I'm suggesting that we stop and consider the brevity of our years on earth, perhaps finding new motivation to preserve the values that will endure. Why should we work ourselves into an early grave, missing those precious moments with loved ones who crave our affection and attention? It is a question that every man and woman should consider.

Let me offer this final word of encouragement for those who are determined to slow the pace: once you get out from under constant pressure, you'll wonder why you drove yourself so hard for all those years. *There is a better way!*

Chapter 11

A Man and His Money

WOULD YOU LIKE to know what Americans think of money and the junk it will buy? Turn on a television set any day at 10:00 A.M., and watch the contestants as they compete for prizes and cash. Observe the coo-coo birds as they leap in the air, frothing at the mouth and tearing at the clothes of the moderator. Notice that their eyes are dilated and their ears are bright pink. It's an unfortunate condition known as *gameshow greed*, and it renders its victims incapable of rational judgment.

Yes, BETTY MOLINO. YOU have won a NEW WASHING MACHINE, a year's supply of CHEWY candy bars, and this marvelous new doll, WANDA WEE-WEE, that actually soaks your daughter's lap. CONGRATULATIONS, Betty, and thanks for playing "GRAB BAG" (frantic applause).

How do I know so much about gameshow greed? Because I've been there! Back in 1967, my lovely wife managed to drag me to the *Let's Make A Deal Show*. Shirley put toy birds all over her head and blouse, and I carried a dumb sign that said, "My wife is for the birds." Really funny, huh? It was good enough for Monty Hall, however, and we were selected as lucky contestants. They placed us in the two front seats near the cameras, but began the program by "dealing" with other suckers.

I kept thinking as I sat in contestants' row, "What in the world am I doing here with this stupid sign?" I couldn't have been more skeptical about the proposition. Finally, Monty called our names and we awaited the verdict.

"Here behind Door #1 is . . . A NEW CAR!" (Audience goes crazy with excitement.)

Suddenly, I was gripped by a spasm in the pit of my stomach. My mouth watered profusely and my heart began knocking on the sides of my chest. There on that stage was the car of my dreams—a brand-new Camaro. Desire came charging up my throat and stuck in the region of my Adam's apple. My breathing became irregular and shallow, which was another unmistakable clue. I had been struck by gameshow greed.

To understand this reaction, you would have to know that I have owned several of the worst cars in automotive history. Throughout my college years I drove a 1949 Mercury convertible that had power seats, power windows, power top, power everything . . . but no power to run them. I put the windows up in the winter and down in the summer. There they remained, despite fluctuating temperatures. Shirley, who was then my girl friend, must have loved me tremendously to have tolerated that car. She *hated* it. The front seat had a spring with bad temper that tore her clothes and punctured her skin. Nor did Ol' Red always choose to run. Shirley spent more than one evening guiding that hunk of scrap iron slowly down the road while I pushed from behind. Talk about hurting your college pride!

The crowning blow occurred shortly after our graduation from college. We were invited to appear for important job interviews and we put on our Sunday best for the occasion. There we were, suit and tie, heels and hose, going sixty miles an hour down the road in Ol' Red, when the top suddenly blew off. Strings and dust flapped us in the face as the canvas waved behind the car like Superman's cape. The ribs of the top protruded above our heads, reminiscent of undersized roll-over bars. And can you believe that Shirley got mad at *me* for letting that happen! She crouched on the floorboard of the car, criticizing me for driving such a beat-up automobile. It is a miracle that our relationship survived that emotional afternoon.

Although Ol' Red had been put to sleep long before the *Let's Make A Deal* experience, I still had never owned a new car. Every available dollar had gone to pay school bills at the University of Southern California in my pursuit of a doctorate, which was earned just two months prior to the television venture.

This explains my reaction to the beautiful automobile behind Door #1.

"All you have to do to win the car," said Monty, "is tell us the prices of these four items." Shirley and I guessed the first three, but the deck was stacked on number four. It was a Hoover portable vacuum cleaner, whose price turned out to be $53.00. We had to guess within $3.00, as I recall. We consulted each other during the commercial break and took a wild shot at $108.00

"Sorry," said Monty Hall. "You've been zonked. But here, take the vacuum cleaner (wow!) and the $3 you won on the other mystery items. And thanks for playing 'Let's Make A Deal.'"

On the way home, Shirley and I talked about how our emotions had been manipulated in that situation. We had both experienced an incredible greed, and the feeling was not comfortable. I have since learned a very valuable lesson about lust and how it operates in a spiritual context. It has been my observation that *whatever* a person hungers for, Satan will appear to offer it in exchange for a spiritual compromise. In my case, a new automobile was the perfect enticement to unleash my greed. But if illicit sex is your desire, it will eventually be made available. Don't be surprised when you are beckoned by a willing partner. If your passion is for fame or power, that object of lust will be promised (even if never delivered). Remember that Jesus was offered bread following His forty-day fast in the wilderness. He was promised power and glory after He had been contemplating His upcoming road to the cross. My point is that Satan uses our keenest appetites to destroy us. Let me repeat the Scripture: "Then when lust hath conceived, it bringeth forth sin: and sin, when it is finished, bringeth forth death" (James 1:15, KJV).

Likewise, if you hunger and thirst after great wealth—beware! Satan's objective is half accomplished already: this materialistic passion is paramount in American society. Someone recently handed me a brochure published by Security Bank in California, which was designed to appeal to a gadget-minded culture. It asked the question, "What do you want to make you happy?" The remaining pages of the pamphlet listed the great sources of joy—a boat, a car, a stove, a television set, and a refrigerator. I wonder if the executives at Security Bank actually believe that happiness can be purchased in the form of an appliance or a vehicle? If so, they should review the words of Jesus, who said, "Take heed, and beware of covetousness: for a man's life consisteth *not* in the abundance of the things which he possesseth" (Luke 12:15, KJV, emphasis added).

Of all the values transmitted to me by my father, none made a more lasting impression than his attitude toward money. As an evangelist, he could never depend on the amount of money he would be given. The local church would collect a free will offering for my father, but many times the gifts were barely sufficient to pay his traveling expenses. Furthermore, he would usually stay with the pastor during a ten-day revival; while there he often observed that the children needed shoes or books or medication. On the final night of the meeting when the modest offering was given to him, my dad would take enough money to get home and then donate the balance to meet the needs of the pastor's family.

Then my dad would return to be greeted by my mother and me. I can still hear the conversations between my good parents.

"Did you have a successful revival?" my mother would ask.

"The Lord was with us," replied my dad.

"How much did they pay you?" she continued.

"Well, I need to talk to you about that," grinned my father.

"I know," said Mom. "You gave it all away, didn't you?"

"Yes, the pastor's kids were so needy and I wanted to help them," he explained.

My mother would invariably sanction his decision, saying if my dad felt that way it was all right. God had always taken good care of us and would continue to do so.

A few days later when the bills began to accumulate, our little family would gather on our knees before the Lord. Dad would pray first.

"Lord, you know we've been faithful with the resources you've given us. We've tried to be responsive to the needs of others when you laid them on our hearts. Now, Lord, *my* family is in need. You've said, 'Give and it shall be given unto you.' So we bring to you our empty meal barrel and ask you to fill it."

As a child, I listened intently to these prayers and watched carefully to see how God responded. I tell you without exaggeration that money invariably arrived in the next few days. God did not make us rich, as some ministers promise today. But He never let us go hungry. On one occasion, $1200 arrived in the mail the day after family prayer. My childlike faith grew by leaps and bounds at this demonstration of trust and sacrifice by my father and mother. I regret that my own children have never seen their parents forced to depend on God in the way I experienced as a boy.

It is interesting to me that Jesus had more to say in the Bible about money than any other subject, which emphasizes the importance of this topic for my family and yours. He made it clear that there is a direct relationship between great riches and spiritual poverty, as we are witnessing in America today. Accordingly, it is my belief that excessive materialism in parents has the power to inflict enormous spiritual damage on our sons and daughters. If they see that we care more about *things* than people . . . if they perceive that we have sought to buy their love as a guilt reducer . . . if they recognize the hollowness of our Christian testimony when it is accompanied by stinginess with God . . . the result is often cynicism and disbelief. And more importantly, when they observe Dad working fifteen hours a day to capture ever more of this world's goods, they *know* where his treasure is. Seeing is believing.

Fathers, it is your responsibility to teach your children Christian attitudes toward possessions and money. It is accomplished not with words, but by the way you handle your own resources. Dr. Mark Lee stated in his book *Creative Christian Marriage,* "A family's value system can be determined from the way they spend money." He is right. It can also be determined from the way the family *doesn't* spend money, since miserliness is also a form of greed.

Let me conclude this discussion by listing fifteen quotations which focus on the subject of money. Two are from my pen and others are Scripture verses or adaptations from various sources. Perhaps you will find them helpful in reinforcing your own system of values.

1. "Everything you own means that much more trouble for you."—Chinese proverb.
2. "The amount of a man's wealth consists in the number of things he can do without."—Ralph Waldo Emerson.
3. "The best way to live happily ever after is not be after too much."—Anonymous.

4. "Desire is like a river. As long as it flows within the banks of God's will—be the current strong or weak—all is well. But when it flows over those boundaries and seeks other channels, then disaster lurks in the rampage."—James Dobson, Sr.

5. "For what shall it profit a man, if he shall gain the whole world, and lose his own soul?"—Jesus, Mark 8:36, KJV.

6. "The only thing you can take to heaven with you is your children (and others you have told about Christ)."—Anonymous.

7. "The love of money is the root of all evil."—1 Timothy 6:10, KJV.

8. "The greatest secret of life is to spend it on something that will outlast it."—Anonymous.

9. "God is entitled to a portion of our income, not because He needs it, but because we need to give it."—James Dobson, Jr.

10. "Why spend your money on foodstuffs that don't give you strength? Why pay for groceries that don't do you any good? Listen and I'll tell you where to get good food that fattens up the soul!"—Isaiah 55:2, TLB.

11. "But they that will be rich fall into temptation and a snare, and into many foolish and hurtful lusts, which drown men in destruction and perdition."—1 Timothy 6:9, KJV.

12. "Such is the human race. Often it does seem a pity that Noah and his party didn't miss the boat."—Mark Twain.

13. "A person brings nothing into this world, and takes nothing out of it. Considering the kind of world it is, he's lucky to break even."—Anonymous.

14. There are said to be seven ages of man.
First age: A child sees the earth.
Second age: He wants it.
Third age: He hustles to get it.
Fourth age: He decides to be satisfied with about half of it.

147

Fifth age: He would be satisfied with less than half of it.
Sixth age: He is now content to possess a two by six foot section of it.
Seventh age: He gets it.   —Anonymous.

15. "I have concluded that the accumulation of wealth, even if I could achieve it, is an insufficient reason for living. When I reach the end of my days, a moment or two from now, I must look backward on something more meaningful than the pursuit of houses and land and machines and stocks and bonds. Nor is fame of any lasting benefit. I will consider my earthly existence to have been wasted unless I can recall a loving family, a consistent investment in the lives of people, and an earnest attempt to serve the God who made me. Nothing else makes much sense." James Dobson, Jr., *What Wives Wish Their Husbands Knew About Women.*

SECTION V

A MAN AND HIS MASCULINITY

Chapter 12

A Man and a Woman and Their Sexual Identity

WE'VE LOOKED AT A man and his children, his wife, and his work. Let's turn our attention now to the man himself and his masculinity. More specifically, I want to examine the changing relationship between the sexes. It is a volatile topic which is guaranteed to raise the reader's blood pressure.

Female sex-role identity has become a major target for change by those who wish to revolutionize the relationship between men and women. The women's movement has, in fact, been remarkably successful in altering the way females "see" themselves at home and in society. In the process, every element of the traditional concept of femininity has been discredited and scorned, especially those responsibilities associated with home-

151

making and motherhood. Thus, in a period of a single decade, the term *housewife* has become a pathetic symbol of exploitation, oppression, and—pardon the insult—stupidity.

Since the beginning of human existence, women in most cultures have identified themselves with child-rearing and nest-building. It was an honorable occupation that required no apology. How has it happened, then, that homemaking has fallen on such lean times in the Western world? Why do women who remain at home in the company of little children feel such disrespect from the society in which they live? A partial answer to these questions can be found in the incessant bombardment by the media on all traditional Judeo-Christian values. Radio, television, the press, and the entertainment industry have literally (and deliberately) changed the way America thinks.

Five years have passed since Barbara Walters and Tom Snyder hosted a three-hour television special on the subject of women. It was aired on NBC in prime time and captured the attention of the country for one full evening. (What fantastic power for social change has been brought by the tube!) I watched Walters and Snyder carefully on that occasion, and, in fact, taped the program for future reference. Their stated purpose was to evaluate the world of women at that time, examining the many activities and involvement of the feminine gender. What resulted, however, was a powerful propaganda piece for the movement. Not once in the three-hour program was the role of the homemaker mentioned, except to refer indirectly to this outmoded responsibility in vaguely derogatory terms. Perhaps 35 million homemakers live and breathe in this country, yet they were not represented once in a program dedicated to the world of women. I'm sure they got the message. That is but one example of how the media bias against traditional femininity has produced the prejudice we now feel.

Have you noticed, also, that the entertainment industry has created a totally new woman with remarkable capacities? We've seen her as Wonder Woman and the Bionic Woman and Spider

Woman and Charlie's Angels and a host of other muscular (but sexy) females. I described their ilk in a previous book, as follows:

The image of women now being depicted by the media is a ridiculous combination of wide-eyed fantasy and feminist propaganda. Today's woman is always shown as gorgeous, of course, but she is more—much more. She roars around the countryside in a racy sports car, while her male companion sits on the other side of the front seat anxiously biting his nails. She exudes self-confidence from the very tips of her fingers, and for good reason: she could dismantle any man alive with her karate chops and flying kicks to the teeth. She is deadly accurate with a pistol and she plays tennis (or football) like a pro. She speaks in perfectly organized sentences, as though her spontaneous remarks were being planned and written by a team of tiny English professors sitting in the back of her pretty head. She is a sexual gourmet, to be sure, but she wouldn't be caught dead in a wedding ceremony. She has the grand good fortune of being perpetually young and she never becomes ill, nor does she ever make a mistake or appear foolish. In short, she is virtually omniscient, except for a curious inability to do anything traditionally feminine, such as cook, sew, or raise children. Truly, today's screen heroine is a remarkable specimen, standing proud and uncompromising, with wide stance and hands on her hips. Oh, yeah! This baby has come a long, long way, no doubt about that. *

My point is that the traditional concept of femininity is being carefully and deliberately dismantled, not only in the minds of adults, but in the world of children, as well. I received a letter recently from a mother who was curious to learn why her local library had removed thousands of books from their shelves. Upon investigation she was shocked to discover that each volume depicting males and females in a traditional context was eliminated. If a mother was shown cooking dinner and a father

---

* *What Wives Wish Their Husbands Knew About Women*, pp. 140–41.

was working in a factory, the book had to go. Obviously, no stone is left unturned in the campaign to change our ideas.

But what has been the result of this unprecedented revolution in feminine sex-role identity? Alas, it has produced a decade of depression and self-doubt among women. God created us as sexual beings, and any confusion in that understanding is devastating to the self-concept. Those most affected are the women who are inextricably identified with the traditional role, those who are "stranded" in a homemaking responsibility. Thus, wives and mothers have found themselves wondering, "Who am I?" and then nervously asking, "Who *should* I be?" It appears that we tore down the old value system before the new one was ready for occupancy, bringing widespread confusion and agitation.

Now a new and surprising phenomenon is taking place. The self-doubt has spread to the masculine gender. I suppose it was inevitable. Any social movement creating chaos in half the population was certain to afflict the other half, sooner or later. As a result, men are now entering the winter of their discontent.

Psychology Today published an article by James Levine in which he reviewed three new books on the subject of manhood in transition. His opening paragraph is indicative of their content:

After countless books about the condition of women that have been published in the last decade, we are now getting a spate of studies about men. *One theme comes through loud and clear: the male is in crisis.* Buffeted by the women's movement, constrained by a traditional and internalized definition of "masculinity," men literally don't know who they are, what women want from them, or even what they want from themselves. *

---

* *Psychology Today*, November 1979, vol. 13 no. 6, p. 147.

It's true. Men *are* in a state of confusion over the meaning of sex-role identity. We know it is unacceptable to be "macho" (whatever in the world that is), but we're a little uncertain about how a real man behaves. Is he a breadwinner and a protector of his family? Well, not exactly. Should he assume a position of leadership and authority at home? Not if he's married to a woman who's had her "consciousness raised." Should he open doors for his wife or give a lady his seat on the train or rise when she enters the room? Who knows? Will he march off to defend his homeland in times of war, or will his wife be the one to fight on foreign soil? Should he wear jewelry and satin shoes or carry a purse? Alas, is there *anything* that marks him as different from his female counterpart? Not to hear the media tell it.

Again, I must make the point that this confused sex-role identity is not the result of random social evolution. It is a product of deliberate efforts to discredit the traditional role of manliness by those who seek *revolution* within the family. Notice that James Levine referred to traditional masculinity as *constraining*. That is precisely how the liberal media and humanistic behavioral scientists perceive the Biblical concept of maleness. Gloria Steinem, expressed it with a bit more venom: "Today, a woman without a man is like a fish without a bicycle."* Frankly, I'm thankful I don't have to spend my life with that fish!

So males and females are in a state of sexual confusion at this time. So what? How does this period of transition affect our future as a nation and as a people? Women's liberationists admit that they aren't sure. Nora Ephron, a feminist staff writer for *Esquire*, responded to the question, "What will happen to sex after the liberation?" She replied, "Frankly, I don't know. It is a great mystery to all of us."**

---

* *Life* magazine, December 1979, p. 140.
** Nora Ephron, "Women," *Esquire*, July 1972:42.

That isn't very comforting. As George Gilder stated in response to Ephron's comment, "Since sex in all its dimensions is the single most important motivating force in human life, what happens to sex after liberation will largely determine what happens to *everything* else. But Ms. Ephron is honest and right. The liberationists have no idea where their program would take us. The movement is counseling us to walk off a cliff, in the evident wish that our society can be kept afloat on feminist hot air." *

Gilder's comment strikes at the heart of the issue. We are sexual beings, and everything that we value is influenced by that aspect of our psychobiology. Whenever that basic nature is tampered with, the stability of society itself is threatened. That is apparently why God placed such specific boundaries on sexual behavior and on the expression of maleness and femaleness. To depart from the prescription is to threaten the entire superstructure of society. Let me ask you to think carefully about the explanation that follows. It is *most* significant.

The book quoted above by George Gilder is entitled *Sexual Suicide,* which I believe to be the most important book written on the relationship between the sexes. In it, he describes the plight of unmarried males and females in the Western world. Women who do not find a mate (or choose not to accept one) are ridiculed as "old maids" or "unclaimed blessings," or similar insulting terms. In other words, they are seen as social misfits in a world of married people. Gilder disagrees. Rather, he says, it is the single *male* who is out of step with society. I'll let Gilder speak for himself.

Men commit over 90 percent of major crimes of violence, 100 percent of the rapes, 95 percent of the burglaries. They comprise 94 percent of our drunken drivers, 70 percent of suicides, 91 percent of

---

* George Gilder, *Sexual Suicide,* Quadrangle/The New York Times Book Company, New York, New York, 1973, p. 7.

offenders against family and children. More specifically, the chief perpetrators are single men. Single men comprise between 80 and 90 percent of most of the categories of social pathology, and on the average they make less money than any other group in the society—yes, less than single women or working women. As any insurance actuary will tell you, single men are also less responsible about their bills, their driving, and other personal conduct. Together with the disintegration of the family, they constitute our leading social problem.

Gilder's point is that the single male is often a threat to society. His aggressive tendencies are largely unbridled and potentially destructive. By contrast, a woman is naturally more motivated to achieve long-term stability. Her maternal inclinations (they *do* exist and are evident in every culture throughout the world) influence her to desire a home and a steady source of income. She wants *security* for herself and her children.

Suddenly, we see the beauty of the divine plan. When a man falls in love with a woman, dedicating himself to care for her and protect her and support her, he suddenly becomes the mainstay of social order. Instead of using his energies to pursue his own lusts and desires, he sweats to build a home and save for the future and seek the best job available. His selfish impulses are inhibited. His sexual passions are channeled. He discovers a sense of pride—yes, masculine pride—because he is needed by his wife and children. Everyone benefits from the relationship.

When a society is composed of millions of individual families that are established on this plan, then the nation is strong and stable. It is the great contribution marriage makes to a civilization. But in its absence, ruination is inevitable. When men have no reason to harness their energies in support of the home, then drug abuse, alcoholism, sexual intrigue, job instability, and aggressive behavior can be expected to run unchecked throughout the culture. And that is the beginning of the end.

Society is not only vulnerable to the sex-role identity of men. Women can also blow it apart. Consider the implications of the declining birth rate in America. It is a woman's prerogative not to have a baby, of course. However, there's something ambiguous about insisting on a "right," which would mean the end of the human race if universally applied! If women wearied of childbearing for a mere thirty-five years on earth, the last generation of mortals would grow old and die, leaving no offspring to reproduce. What godlike power is possessed by the female of the species! She can take the bit in her mouth and gallop down the road to oblivion with a wagonload of humanity bumping along behind. No hydrogen bomb could destroy us more effectively, without bloodshed or pollution.

But this is not merely a bad dream with no basis in reality. For several years, it has been almost impossible to find anything positive written about human babies in liberal and leftist publications. Kids have been perceived as an imposition, a nuisance, and a drain on the world's natural resources. They're seen as part of the "population bomb" that supposedly plagues the earth. I'm convinced that this negative bias plays a role in the epidemic of child abuse that rages throughout this country. It is certainly related to the shameful abortion phenomenon occurring during the past decade. More than a million American babies are now aborted annually (55 million worldwide), infants who will never take their place in the fabric of our society. What remains is an aging population with fewer children to step into our shoes. What will happen if the present generation reaches retirement age and still outnumbers the younger workers? Who would support the social security system when today's adults become too old to earn a living? Who would populate the military when America is threatened from abroad? What would happen to an economy that is based on decreasing returns rather than growth and productivity? Yes, the liberated woman will have had her way—her "right" to abortion and childlessness. She will have proved that no one could tell her what to do with her body. But what a victory!

I've written this entire chapter to convey one simple message. We *must* not abandon the Biblical concept of masculinity and femininity at this delicate stage of our national history. Not that every woman must become a mother, mind you, or even a homemaker. But those who *do* must be honored and respected and supported. There should be a clear delineation between maleness and femaleness, exemplified by clothing, customs, and function. Children must be valued as our most priceless possession. They should be taught that the sexes are equal in worth, but very different from one another. Girls should know they are girls and boys should know they are boys. And for the rest of us, self-awareness begins with an understanding of our sexual identity. It must not be blurred by the forces of revolution that rage around us.

Chapter 13

A Man and a Woman and Their Biological Differences

THE PREVIOUS CHAPTER was devoted to the importance of maintaining male and female sex roles as separate entities. In other words, I attempted to explain why men and women should *behave* differently. Before leaving that general subject, however, I would like to offer some evidence to show that men and women are biologically unique. The women's movement, in its assault on traditional sex roles, has repeatedly asserted that males and females are identical except for the ability to bear children. Nothing could be farther from the truth.

Let's begin by discussing the human brain, where maleness and femaleness are rooted. Careful research is revealing that the basic differences between the sexes are neurological in origin,

160

rather than being purely cultural as ordinarily presumed. As Dr. Richard Restak stated in his book, *The Brain: The Last Frontier:* *

> Certainly, anyone who has spent time with children in a playground or school setting is aware of the differences in the way boys and girls respond to similar situations. Think of the last time you supervised a birthday party attended by five-year-olds. It's not usually the girls who pull hair, throw punches, or smear each other with food. Usually such differences are explained on a cultural basis. Boys are expected to be more aggressive and play rough games, while girls are presumably encouraged to be more gentle, nonassertive, and passive. After several years of exposure to such expectations, so the theory goes, men and women wind up with widely varying behavioral and intellectual repertoires. As a corollary to this, many people believe that if child-rearing practices could be equalized and sexual-role stereotypes eliminated, most of these differences would eventually disappear. As often happens, however, the true state of affairs is not that simple.
>
> Recent psychological research indicates that many of the differences in brain function between the sexes are innate, biologically determined, and relatively resistant to change through the influences of culture. (p. 197)

Dr. Restak presents numerous studies that document this statement, and then concludes this chapter by quoting Dr. David Wechsler, creator of the most popular intelligence test for use with adults.

> ". . . our findings do confirm what poets and novelists have often asserted, and the average layman long believed, namely, that men not only behave but 'think' differently from women." (p. 206)

Both Drs. Restak and Wechsler are right. Males and females differ anatomically, sexually, emotionally, psychologically, and

---

* Garden City, NY: Doubleday & Company, 1979.

biochemically. We differ in literally every cell of our bodies, for each sex carries a unique chromosomal pattern. Much is written today about so-called sex-change operations, whereby males are transformed into females or vice versa. Admittedly, it is possible to alter the external genitalia by surgery, and silicone can be used to pad the breasts or round out a bony frame. Hormones can then be injected to feminize or masculinize the convert. But nothing can be done to change the assignment of sex made by God at the instant of conception. That determination is carried in each cell, and it will read "male" or "female" from the earliest moment of life to the point of death. The Bible says emphatically, "Male *and* female created he them" (Gen. 1:27, KJV, emphasis added). Not one sex, but *two!*

Furthermore, it is my deep conviction that each sex displays unique emotional characteristics that are genetically endowed. Cultural influences cannot account for these novelties. Few psychologists have had the courage to express this view in recent years, because the women's movement has perceived it as insulting. But to be *different* from men does not make women *inferior* to men. Males and females are original creations of God, each bearing strengths and weaknesses that counterbalance and interface with one another. It is a beautiful design that must not be disassembled.

Just how do female emotions differ from those of males? Let's consider first the importance of the menstrual cycle. I'm reminded of the late 1960s when hairy young men and women became almost undistinguishable from each other. Two of these hippies, a male and female, were involved in a minor traffic accident and were taken to a local hospital for treatment. The nurse who was completing the intake forms could not determine from their clothing and appearance which sex they represented. After considering the dilemma for a moment she asked, "Okay, which one of you has a menstrual cycle?"

The hippie with the bass voice looked at her through his bangs and said. "Not me, man. I gots a Honda."

The question was more significant than merely determining the sex of the patients. Included in this matter of menstruation are many implications for the way females feel about life during the course of the month. It has been said, quite accurately, that the four weeks of the menstrual cycle are characteristic of the four seasons of the year. The first week after a period can be termed the springtime of the physiological calendar. New estrogens (female hormones) are released each day and a woman's body begins to rebound from the recent winter.

The second week represents the summertime of the cycle, when the living is easy. A woman during this phase has more self-confidence than during any other phase of the month. It is a time of maximum energy, enthusiasm, amiability, and self-esteem. Estrogen levels account for much of this optimism, reaching a peak during mid-cycle when ovulation occurs. The relationship between husband and wife is typically at its best during these days of summer, when sexual desire (and the potential for pregnancy) are paramount.

But alas, the fall must surely follow summer. Estrogen levels steadily dwindle as the woman's body prepares itself for another period of menstruation. A second hormone, called pro-gesterone, is released, which reduces the effect of estrogen and initiates the symptoms of premenstrual tension. It is a bleak phase of the month. Self-esteem deteriorates day by day, bringing depression and pessimism with it. A bloated and sluggish feeling often produces not only discomfort but also the belief that "I am ugly." Irritability and aggression become increasingly evident as the week progresses, reaching a climax immediately prior to menstruation.

Then come the winter and the period of the menstrual flow. Women differ remarkably in intensity of these symptoms, but most experience some discomfort. Those most vulnerable even find it necessary to spend a day or two in bed during the winter season, suffering from cramping and generalized misery. Gradually, the siege passes and the refreshing newness of springtime returns.

163

How can anyone who understands this cyclical pattern contend that there are no genetically determined psychological differences between males and females? No such system operates in men. The effect of the menstrual cycle is not only observable clinically, but it can be documented statistically.

The incidences of suicides, homicides, and infanticides perpetrated by women are significantly higher during the period of premenstrual tension than any other phase of the month. Consider also the findings of Alec Coppen and Neil Kessel, who studied 465 women and observed that they were more irritable and depressed during the premenstrual phase than during mid-cycle. "This was true for neurotic, psychotic and normal women alike. Similarly Natalie Sharness found the pre-menstrual phase associated with feelings of helplessness, anxiety, hostility, and yearning for love. At menstruation, this tension and irritability eased, but depression often accompanied the relief, and lingered until estrogen increased." *

I doubt that these facts will come as a great revelation to men or women. Both sexes know that behavior and attitudes are related to the monthly pattern. I receive interesting letters from men who ask, "How can I cope with my wife's irritability during this phase?" Their question reminds me of an incident shared with me by my friend Dr. David Hernandez, who is an obstetrician and gynecologist in private practice. The true story involves Latin men whose wives were given birth control pills by a pharmaceutical company. The Federal Drug Administration in America would not permit hormonal research to be conducted, so the company selected a small fishing village in South America which agreed to cooperate. All the women in the town were given the pill on the same date, and after three weeks the prescription was terminated to permit menstruation. That meant, of course, that every adult female in the community was

---

* *Psychology Today,* February 1972.

experiencing premenstrual tension at the same time. The men couldn't take it. They all headed for their boats each month and remained at sea until the crisis passed at home. They knew, even if militant liberationists don't, that females are different from males . . . especially every twenty-eight days.

But there are other ways women are unique. Female emotions are also influenced by two other exclusively feminine functions, lactation and pregnancy. Furthermore, the hypothalamus, which is located at the base of the brain and has been called the "seat of the emotions," is apparently wired very differently for males than females. For example, a severe emotional shock or trauma can be interpreted by the hypothalmus, which then sends messages to the pituitary by way of neurons and hormones. The pituitary often responds by changing the body chemistry of the woman, perhaps interrupting the normal menstrual cycle for six months or longer. Female physiology is a finely tuned instrument, being more vulnerable and complex than the masculine counterpart. Why some women find that fact insulting is still a mystery to me.

How do these differences translate into observable behavior? Medical science has not begun to identify all the ramifications of sexual uniqueness. Some of the implications are extremely subtle. For example, when researchers quietly walked on high school and college campuses to study behavior of the sexes, they observed that males and females even transported their books in different ways. The young men tended to carry them at their sides with their arms looped over the top. Women and girls, by contrast, usually cradled their books at their breasts, in much the same way they would a baby. Who can estimate how many other sex-related influences lie below the level of consciousness?

Admittedly, some of the observed differences between the sexes *are* culturally produced. I don't know how to sort out those which are exclusively genetic from those which represent learned responses. Frankly, it doesn't seem to matter a great deal. The differences exist, for whatever reason, and the current cultural revolution will not alter most of them significantly. At the risk of being called a sexist, or a propagator of sexual stereotypes, or a male chauvinist pig (or worse), let me delineate a few of the emotional patterns typical of women as compared with men.

1. As stated in the previous chapter, the reproductive capacity of women results in a greater appreciation for stability, security, and enduring human relationships. In other words, females are more *future*-oriented because of their concern for children.

2. Related to the first item is a woman's emotional investment in her home, which usually exceeds that of her husband. She typically cares more than he about the minor details of the house, family functioning, and such concerns. To cite a personal example, my wife and I decided to install a new gas barbecue unit in our back yard. When the plumber completed the assignment and departed, Shirley and I both recognized that he had placed the appliance approximately six inches too high. I looked at the device and said, "Hmmm, yes sir, he sure made a mistake. That post is a bit too high. By the way, what are we having for dinner tonight?" Shirley's reaction was dramatically different. She said, "The plumber has that thing sticking up in the air and I don't think I can stand it!" Our contrasting views represented a classic difference of emotional intensity relating to the home.

3. Anyone who doubts that males and females are unique should observe how they approach a game of Ping Pong or Monopoly or dominoes or horseshoes or volleyball or tennis. Women often use the event as an excuse for fellowship and pleasant conversation. For men, the name of the game is *conquest*. Even if the setting is a friendly social gathering in the host's backyard, the beads of sweat on each man's forehead reveal his passion to win. This aggressive competitiveness has

been attributed to cultural influences. I don't believe it. As Richard Restak said, "At a birthday party for five-year-olds, it's not usually the girls who pull hair, throw punches, or smear each other with food."

4. Males and females apparently differ in the manner by which they develop self-esteem. Men draw the necessary evidence of their worthiness primarily from their jobs—from being respected in business, profession or craft. Women, however, *especially those who are homemakers*, depend primarily on the romantic relationship with their husbands for ego support. This explains why the emotional content of a marriage is often of greater significance to women than men and why tokens of affection are appreciated more by wives, who obtain esteem from these expressions of love and generosity.

5. A maternal instinct apparently operates in most women, although its force is stronger in some than others. This desire to procreate is certainly evident in those who are unable to conceive. I receive a steady influx of letters from women who express great frustration from their inability to become mothers. Although culture plays a major role in these longings, I believe they are rooted in female anatomy and physiology.

6. Perhaps the most dramatic differences between males and females are evident in their contrasting sexual preferences. He is more visually oriented, caring less about the romantic component. She is attracted not to a photograph of an unknown model or by a handsome stranger, but to a *particular* man with whom she has entered into an emotional relationship. This differing orientation is merely the tip of the iceberg in delineating the sexual uniqueness of males and females.

These items are illustrative and are not intended to represent a scientific delineation of sexual differences. The reader is invited to add his own observations to the list and to make his own interpretations.

Conclusion

As a summary to these chapters dealing with male and female identities, let me offer two *opinions* with regard to masculine leadership. They are as follows:

1. Because of the fragile nature of the male ego and a man's enormous need to be respected, combined with female vulnerability and a woman's need to be loved, I feel it is a mistake to tamper with the time-honored relationship of husband as loving protector and wife as recipient of that protection.

2. Because two captains sink the ship and two cooks spoil the broth, I feel that a family must have a leader whose decisions prevail in times of differing opinions. If I understand the Scriptures, that role has been assigned to the man of the house. However, he must not incite his crew to mutiny by heavy-handed disregard for their feelings and needs. He should, in fact, put the best interests of his family above his own, even to the point of death, if necessary. Nowhere in Scripture is he authorized to become a dictator or slave-owner.

Other combinations of husband-wife teamwork have been successful in individual families, but I've seen many complications occurring in marriages where the man was passive, weak, and lacking in qualities of leadership. None of the modern alternatives have improved on the traditional, masculine role as prescribed in the Good Book. It was, after all, inspired by the Creator of mankind.

If this be macho, sexist, chauvinist, and stereotypical, then I'm guilty as charged. (Please address all hate mail to my secretary, who has a special file prepared for it.)

SECTION VI

A MAN AND HIS EMOTIONS

Chapter 14

A Man and His Mid-Life Years

THE LATE Bishop Fulton Sheen reported entering a greasy spoon restaurant for breakfast one morning. The waitress, who seemed half asleep, asked what he wanted to eat.

"Bring me some ham and eggs and a few kind words for the day," he said.

She returned fifteen minutes later and set the food before him. "There," she said.

"What about the kind words?" he asked.

The waitress looked him over for a moment and then replied, "I'd advise you not to eat them eggs!"

On some occasions it seems impossible to get a kind word from anyone. The first few events of the morning make it clear that bad news is coming down the pike, and there's no stopping it. Someone with a great sense of humor described a few of those circumstances that let us know "it's gonna be a bad day when . . ."

1. You wake up face down on the pavement.
2. You call Suicide Prevention and they put you on hold.
3. You see a "60 Minutes News Team" waiting in your office.
4. Your birthday cake collapses from the weight of the candles.
5. You turn on the news and they're displaying emergency routes out of your city.
6. Your twin sister forgets your birthday.
7. You wake up to discover that your water bed broke and then you realize that you don't have a water bed.
8. You're following a group of Hell's Angels down the freeway when suddenly your horn goes off and remains stuck.

We smile at these exaggerations because they hit so close to home. Every member of the human family has gone through bad days when frustration and irritation seemed to rain from the sky. For some individuals, however, these difficult days arrive in bunches and continue for months. In fact, I have devoted the balance of this chapter to a period in a man's life when bad days typically outnumber the good. It is a stressful era known as the "mid-life years." During this time of transition, a man may feel *every* morning as though he spent the night lying face down in the gutter.

To explain the meaning of mid-life crisis, let's first consider a child at the moment of birth. Though he has just arrived on the scene, a great deal can be anticipated about his next twenty years. We can predict, with a high degree of accuracy, that he will experience most of the same periods of stress and conflict that other boys and girls have encountered. He'll toddle through the terrible twos, then glide into the more tranquil elementary school years before being besieged by puberty. The period of early adolescence is likely to be stormy, followed a few years later by the frightening experience of leaving home. This perilous journey from birth to adulthood has been studied exhaustively and mapped inch by inch. There are very few surprises within the science of child development today.

However, we have only recently begun to recognize that *adulthood* is also characterized by predictable periods of tranquility and stress. The journey is not as well charted for men and women as it has been for children, of course, but the map is beginning to take shape. It is now apparent that the mature years continue to be characterized by alternating periods of equilibrium and disequilibrium, and that the human experience offers remarkable similarities from person to person. The Apostle Paul referred to this commonality when he wrote, "There hath no temptation taken you but such as is common to man." (1 Cor. 10:13, KJV).

Other books have attempted to map the entire journey from youth to old age, (i.e., *Passages* by Gail Sheehy, and *Stages* by John Claypool). Our concern here will be limited to that brief sketch of road known as the mid-life years, which can be particularly bumpy for everyone on board. Both males and females can expect to be jostled and jarred while traveling that unpaved section of the highway. Women experience these stresses during the disequilibrium of menopause, when reproductive activity is waning. I once heard comedienne Erma Bombeck asked to reveal her age on a television talk show. She replied, "I'm somewhere between estrogen and death." I know many menopausal women who feel they hang between those alternatives today.*

For this discussion, however, our emphasis will be on the *male* in mid-life crisis. It is a vitally important topic, especially to those men who are approaching their third and fourth (or possibly fifth) decades on this earth. Lee Stockford reported the findings of three studies involving more than 2100 persons and concluded that 80 percent of the executives between 34 and 42

---

* I discussed the symptoms and treatment of menopause in *What Wives Wish Their Husbands Knew About Women.*

years of age experience a mid-life trauma of some variety. This estimate is consistent with my own observations, especially among highly motivated, successful business and professional men.

To men and their wives who want a better understanding of the stresses I've described, I enthusiastically recommend Jim Conway's excellent book, *Men in Mid-Life Crisis*. Dr. Conway is a minister who went through his own mid-life nightmare and survived to tell the story. His book is the best I have read on the subject and will be helpful to those who have reached that stage of their journey.

After Conway's book came to my attention, I devoted two radio programs (broadcast on 140 stations) to its theme. A literal avalanche of mail and phone calls poured into my office the following month. Men wrote to say, "I am there," and wives asked, "How can I help my husband through this awful experience?"

With Dr. Conway's permission, I have chosen to review the major concepts from his book * and then add my own suggestions and interpretations. Let's begin with the basic question, "What is a mid-life crisis." It is a time of intense personal evaluation when frightening and disturbing thoughts surge through the mind, posing questions about who I am and why I'm here and what it all matters. It is a period of self-doubt and disenchantment with everything familiar and stable. It represents terrifying thoughts that can't be admitted or revealed even to those closest to us. These anxieties often produce an uncomfortable separation between loved ones at a time when support and understanding are desperately needed.

Conway identifies four major "enemies" which plague a man entering his mid-life years. The first is his own body. There is no doubt about it; that guy they called "Joe College" just a few years ago is now growing older. His hair is falling out, despite desperate attempts to coddle and protect every remaining

---

* The following discussion excerpted from *Men in Mid-Life Crisis* by Jim Conway, © 1978 David C. Cook Publishing Co., Elgin, IL 60120. Used by permission.

strand. "Me, bald?" he shudders. Then he notices he doesn't have the stamina he once had. He begins getting winded on escalators. Before long, words assume new meanings for Ol' Joe. "The rolling stones" are in his gall bladder and "speed" (which once referred to amphetamines or fast driving) is his word for prune juice. He takes a business trip and the stewardess offers him "coffee, tea, or milk of magnesia." The cells in his face then pack up and run south for the winter, leaving a shocked and depressed Joseph standing two inches from the mirror in disbelief.

I'm kidding, of course, but not much. If you think only women get depressed over evidence of aging, then you know little about the male of the species. It is severely disturbing to most men to realize they will soon lose their appeal to the opposite sex . . . that physical power and vitality are declining . . . that the golden age of youth has come and gone. This awareness becomes undeniable during the period between thirty-five and forty years of age. Until then, an athletic man can still compete in basketball or tennis or baseball with his younger friends. But suddenly, for reasons which I can't explain, the deterioration becomes more noticeable in this Valley of the Shadow. Those who disagree have simply been too busy to recognize the decline. Even the best and most durable of professional athletes usually end their careers in their thirty-sixth or thirty-seventh years, not by choice but by the onset of huffing and puffing.

Consider the record of Muhammad Ali, who was the world heavyweight boxing champion at thirty-five, but had been whipped by a boy (Leon Spinks) at thirty-six and was retired at thirty-seven. Jerry West and John Havlicek, who at thirty-five were two of the best guards in NBA history, were both out of business at thirty-seven. The pattern is repeated dozens of times every year. A superstar who consistently wowed the fans *suddenly* gets too old to compete. And another jock waves goodbye to the crowd.

Those of us who earn our living in nonathletic pursuits are

less vulnerable to aging, but deep inside we also know things are changing. Our fathers often experience their first cardiac problems when we are in our middle decades, which makes us nervous about the time bombs ticking within our own chests. A deodorant commercial asks, "Where will you be when it stops working?" Every middle-aged man has posed that question about his heart.

To summarize this first great concern of the mid-life years, a man approaching forty is forced to admit (1) he is getting older; (2) the changes produced by aging are neither attractive nor convenient; (3) in a world that equates human worth with youth and beauty, he is about to suffer a personal devaluation; and (4) old age is less than two decades away, bringing eventual sickness and death. When a man confronts this package for the first time, he is certain to experience an emotional reverberation from its impact.

The second enemy facing a man in his mid-life years is his work. He typically resents his job and feels trapped in the field he has chosen. Many blue- and white-collar workers wish they'd had the opportunity to study medicine or law or dentistry. Little do they realize that physicians and attorneys and orthodontists often wish they had selected less demanding occupations . . . jobs that could be forgotten on evenings and weekends . . . jobs that didn't impose the constant threat of malpractice suits . . . jobs that left time for recreation and hobbies. This occupational unrest at all socioeconomic levels reaches a peak of intensity in the middle years, when the new awareness of life's brevity makes men reluctant to squander a single day that remains. But, on the other hand, they have little choice. The financial needs of their families demand that they keep pressing . . . so the kids can go to college . . . so the house payment can be met . . . so the lives they have known can continue. Thus, their emotions are caught in an ever-tightening vise.

A man's common reaction to this frustration is to seek an escape. Some husbands run away without telling their loved ones where they're going. Others make a radical change in employment, perhaps losing years of retirement benefits or seniority. But the majority hang tough. They just complain and get depressed and threaten to quit . . . but they'll be on the job tomorrow morning. If you listen closely you'll hear them mutter, "I don't wanna but I gotta!"

We should consider one other aspect of a man's work during his mid-life years, relating to his dreams. When he was young, he fully expected to be the President, or at least a millionaire by the time he was thirty. But as time begins to run out, he realizes not only that he'll never achieve his fantasy, but that his *present* accomplishment probably represents the high-water mark for his life. Yes, Virginia, *this* is it! We can easily see why Conway identified a man's work as his enemy during this period of transition.

The third enemy that rises to confront a middle-aged man is, believe it or not, his own family. These stormy years of self-doubt and introspection can be devastating to marriage. Such a man often becomes angry and depressed and rebellious toward those closest to him. He resents the fact that his wife and kids need him. No matter how hard he works, they always require more money than he can earn, and that agitates him further. At a time when he is in a selfish mood, wanting to meet his own needs, it seems that every member of the family is pulling on him. Even his parents have now become his financial and emotional responsibility. Again, he is seized by the urge to run.

At this delicate point in a man's life, Satan reaches into his ugly bag of tricks and retrieves the most foul of all his suggestions: adultery. What a vile alternative to plant in the troubled mind of a husband and father at this time of disenchantment. That pretty little secretary, who has serious emotional needs of her own, possesses enormous power to soothe his wounds and patch his pride. She offers the ultimate escape from the entrapment of mid-life. But what a price she and her lover will pay for their illicit adventure. When their fling has run its course, they must face the spouses they have betrayed and the children they have abandoned and the God they have disobeyed. The consequences of their sin will reverberate through eternity, hurting the innocent as certainly as the guilty.

Conway informs us that King David's affair with Bathsheba, leading ultimately to the murder of her husband, actually began with a severe mid-life crisis. Indeed, David's writings do reveal the classic struggles of a middle-aged man. He wrote in Psalms: "for my days disappear like smoke. . . . My life is passing swiftly as the evening shadows. I am withering like grass. . . . He has cut me down in middle life, shortening my days" (Ps. 102:3, 11, 23, TLB).

At this point of vulnerability, David, who was on the roof, happened to see Bathsheba as she bathed. The rest of the sordid story is history. It was to be the one black mark on David's record, according to the unflinching assessment written in 1 Kings 15:5 (TLB): "For David had obeyed God during his entire life except for the affair concerning Uriah the Hittite" (Uriah was Bathsheba's husband whom David murdered after learning of her pregnancy).

It is important to understand that David and Bathsheba fell into this sin because they were *ripe* for an affair. David, who had literally hundreds of wives and concubines, was entitled to possess any unmarried woman in the land. Instead, he wanted Uriah's wife—not because *she* was different, but because *he* was different. His damaged ego needed what she could offer at that precise time. And as for Bathsheba, remember that her husband was away at war. She was probably lonely and depressed on that night of passion. Why else was she bathing in full view of the king?

Conway's point, which is undeniable, is that a man and woman commit adultery when they are emotionally *ready* for it. As he said, "Invariably, a set of circumstances sets them up, like

David, and they think of the affair as a way to satisfy the discontent they feel." Let the reader beware.

The fourth and final enemy of a man in mid-life crisis appears to be God Himself. Through a strange manipulation of logic, man blames the Creator for all his troubles, approaching Him with rebellion and anger. In return, he feels condemned and abandoned and unloved by God. The consequence is a weakened faith and a crumbling system of beliefs. This explains, more than any other factor, the radical changes in behavior that often accompany the struggles of middle life.

Let me give this latter point the strongest possible emphasis. One of the most common observations made by relatives and friends of a man in mid-life crisis reflects this sudden reversal of personality and behavior.

"I don't understand what happened to Loren," a wife will say. "He seemed to change overnight from a stable, loving husband and father to an irresponsible rogue. He quit going to church. He began openly flirting with other women. He lost interest in our sons. Even his clothing became modish and flamboyant. He started combing his hair forward to hide his baldness and he bought a new sports car that we couldn't afford. I just can't figure out what suddenly came over my dependable husband."

This man has obviously experienced the changes we have described, but his *basic* problem is spiritual in nature. As his system of beliefs disintegrated, then his commitment to related Biblical concepts was weakened accordingly. Monogamy, fidelity, responsibility, life after death, self-denial, Christian witnessing, basic honesty, and dozens of other components of his former faith suddenly became invalid or suspect. The result was a rapid and catastrophic change in lifestyles which left his family and friends in a state of confusion and shock. This pattern has occurred for thousands of families in recent years.

Let's turn our attention now from a description of the problem to a few suggestions for those who have experienced these difficulties. Returning to my prior recommendation, I would urge everyone (male and female) to read Conway's book. He devoted a 300-page manuscript to a topic I could only address in a single chapter. In the final pages of *Men In Mid-Life Crisis*, Conway lists ten suggestions under the heading "What seemed to help me." There he discusses the therapeutic value of exercise, new challenges, music, talking, rest, Bible reading and prayer in reestablishing one's equilibrium. I will not repeat those concepts here, choosing instead to emphasize two factors which Conway may have understated.

First, I want to give *hope* directly to the man in mid-life crisis. Just as behavioral scientists were able to predict that you would journey into this troubling era, we can also anticipate your emergence from it. An analogy to adolescence is helpful at this point: both periods are relatively short-term, age-related times of transition which produce intense anxiety, self-doubt, introspection, and agitation. Fortunately, however, neither adolescence nor the mid-life years represent permanent traps which hold victims captive. Rather, they can be thought of as doors through which we must all pass and from which we will all emerge. What I'm saying is that *normality will return* (unless you make some disruptive mistakes in a desperate attempt to cope).

Second, I feel the need to stress what I consider to be *the* fundamental cause of a mid-life crisis. It results from what the Bible refers to as "building your house upon the sand." It is possible to be a follower of Jesus Christ and accept His forgiveness from Sin, yet still be deeply influenced by the values and attitudes of one's surrounding culture. Thus, a young Christian husband and father may become a workaholic, a hoarder of money, a status-seeker, a worshiper of youth, and a lover of pleasure. These tendencies may not reflect his conscious choices and desires; they merely represent the stamp of society's godless values on his life and times.

Despite his unchristian attitudes, the man may appear to "have it all together" in his first fifteen years as an adult, especially if he is successful in early business pursuits. But he is in considerable danger. Whenever we build our lives on values and principles that contradict the time-honored wisdom of God's Word, we are laying a foundation on the sand. Sooner or later, the storms will howl and the structure we have laboriously constructed will collapse with a mighty crash.

Stated succinctly, a mid-life crisis is more likely to be severe for those whose values reflect the temporal perspectives of this world. A man does not mourn the loss of his youth, for example, if he honestly believes that his life is merely a preparation for a better one to follow. And God does not become the enemy of a man who has walked and talked with Him in daily communion and love. And the relationship between a man and his wife is less strained in the mid-life years if they have protected and maintained their friendship since they were newlyweds. In short, the mid-life crisis represents a day of reckoning for a lifetime of wrong values, unworthy goals, and ungodly attitudes.

Perhaps this explains my observation that most men in the throes of a mid-life crisis are long-term workaholics. They have built their mighty castles on the sandy beach of materialism, depending on money and status and advancement and success to meet all their needs. They reserved no time for wife, children, friends or God. Drive! Push! Hustle! Scheme! Invest! Prepare! Anticipate! Work! Fourteen-hour days were followed by week-ends at the office and forfeited vacations and midnight oil. Then after twenty years of this distorted existence, they suddenly have cause to question the value of it all. "Is this really what I want to do with my life?" they ask. They realize too late that they have frantically climbed the ladder of success, only to discover that it was leaning against the wrong wall.

Perhaps the reader now understands why I have attacked this overcommitted lifestyle throughout my book. In the American system, it is the villain that destroys marriage, Christian devotion, emotional health, and the well-being of children. In my opinion, overwork is the sour note in the symphony of

American values. It can even make a forty-year-old man want to run and hide.

> Across the fields of yesterday
> He sometimes comes to me
> A little lad just back from play
> The boy I used to be
>
> He smiles at me so wistfully
> When once he's crept within
> It is as though he had hoped to see
> The man I might have been.

Author unknown

Chapter 15

A Man and His Emotions

HAVE YOU EVER stood outdoors near the end of a day and heard the whining sound of a mosquito flying past your ear?

"I'll bet I'm about to get punctured," you think.

Just then, you feel the creature light on your forearm and you immediately glance downward. But to your surprise, the insect is not there. You merely imagined that you had been invaded.

Or in another context, have you ever awakened after a frightening dream, lying breathless in your bed? You listened to the sounds of the night, wondering if the dream was based on reality. Then suddenly, just as you expected, there was a "bump" coming from the dark side of the house. An hour later you concluded that no one was actually there.

Emotions are powerful forces within the human mind. Fear, especially, has a remarkable way of generating evidence to support itself. Physicians in clinical practice spend a large portion of their time convincing people that their self-diagnoses are not accurate, that their symptoms are imaginary or psychosomatic.

Even the young and the brave experience such deception. My good friend Steve Smith won a bronze star for courage in Vietnam combat. However, the first night his unit arrived in the war-torn country was not to be remembered for remarkable valor. His company had never seen actual combat, and the men were terrified. They dug foxholes on a hill and nervously watched the sun disappear beyond the horizon. At approximately midnight, the enemy attacked as anticipated. Guns began to blaze on one side of the mountain, and before long all the soldiers were firing frantically and throwing hand grenades into the darkness. The battle raged throughout the night and the infantry appeared to be winning. Finally, the long-awaited sun came up and the body count began. But not one single dead Viet Cong lay at the perimeter of the mountain. In fact, not one enemy soldier had even participated in the attack. The company of green troops had fought the night in mortal combat . . . and won.

Permit me one further example of emotions that overruled reason. The city of Los Angeles was paralyzed with fear in 1969, when Charles Manson and his "family" murdered Sharon Tate and her friends and then butchered Leno and Rosemary La Bianca in cold blood. Residents wondered who would be next. My mother was quite convinced that she was the prime candidate. Sure enough, Mom and Dad heard the intruder as they lay in bed one night. "Thump!" went the sound from the area of the kitchen.

"Did you hear that?" asked my mother.

"Yes, be quiet," said my father.

They lay staring at the darkened ceiling, breathing shallowly and listening for further clues. A second "thump" brought them to their feet. They felt their way to the bedroom door, which was closed. At this point, we are shown a vast difference between how my mother and my father faced a crisis. Mom's inclination was to hold the door shut to keep the intruder from entering the bedroom. Thus, she propped her foot against the bottom of the door and threw her weight against the upper section. My father's approach was to confront the attacker head on. He reached through the darkness and grasped the doorknob, but his pull met the resistance from my mother.

My father assumed someone was holding the door shut from the other side. My terrified mother, on the other hand, could feel the killer trying to force the door open. My parents stood there in the pitch blackness of midnight, struggling against one another and imagining themselves to be in a tug of war with a murderer. Mother then decided to abandon ship. She released the door and ran to the window to scream at the top of her lungs. She took a great breath of air with which to summon the entire city of Pasadena, when she realized a light was on behind her. Turning around, she saw that my dad had gone into the other part of the house in search of their attacker. Obviously, he was able to open the door when she released it. In reality, there was no prowler. The thumps were never identified and Charles Manson never made his anticipated visit.

Let me personalize the issue at hand. What imaginary fears are *you* supporting with contrived evidence? What role do rampant, uncontrolled emotions play in your life? It is likely that what you feel, right or wrong, is a powerful force in determining your behavior day by day. Emotional experience in the Western world has become *the* primary motivation of values and actions and even spiritual beliefs. Furthermore (and this is the point), we are living in a day when we are being encouraged to release our emotions . . . to grant them even greater power in ruling our destinies. We are told, "If it feels good, do it!" The popular song "You Light Up My Life" carries this phrase, "It can't be wrong, 'cause it *feels* so right." (Hitler's murder of the Jews probably felt right to the Nazis at the time.) Most love songs, in fact, make it clear that a commitment to one another is based on the excitement the couple shares. Thus, when the thrill evaporates, so does the relationship. By contrast, the greatest piece of literature ever written on the subject of love, the 13th chapter of 1 Corinthians, includes not a single reference to feelings: "Love is very patient and kind, never jealous or envious, never boastful or proud, never haughty or selfish or rude. Love does not demand its own way. It is not irritable or touchy. It does not hold grudges and will hardly even notice when others do it wrong" (1 Cor. 13:4–5, TLB).

It is my opinion that we should take a long, hard look at the "Discovery of Personhood," which seeks to free our emotions from restraint and inhibition. This pop-psyche movement, so prevalent in San Francisco and other California cities, encourages us to get in touch with our feelings . . . to open up . . . to tell it like it is. We've come through an emphasis on "encounter groups," where participants were urged to attack one another and cry and scream and remove their clothes and even whack each other with foamy "encounter bats." Great stuff.

I have no desire to return our culture to the formality of yesterday, when father was a marble statue and mother couldn't smile because her corset was too tight. But if our grandparents represented one extreme of emotional repression, today's Americans have become temperamental yo-yos at the other. We live and breathe by the vicissitudes of our feelings, and for many, the depression of the "lows" is significantly more prevalent than the elation of the "highs." Reason is now *dominated* by feelings, rather than the reverse, as God intended. "But when the Holy Spirit controls our lives he will produce this kind of fruit in us: love, joy, peace, patience, kindness, goodness, faithfulness, gentleness and *self-control*" (Gal. 5:22, TLB, emphasis added).

This need for *self-control* is emphasized by the difficulties and stresses that occur in the lives of virtually every human being on earth. As Mark Twain said, "Life is just one darn thing after another." It's true. At least once every two weeks, someone gets a chest cold or the roof springs a leak or the car throws a rod or an ingrown toenail becomes infected or a business crisis develops. Those minor frustrations are inevitable. In time, of course, more significant problems develop. Loved ones die and catastrophic diseases appear and life slowly grinds to a conclusion. This is the nature of human experience, whether we like it or not. That being true, nothing could be more dangerous than to permit our emotions to rule our destinies. To do so is to be cast adrift in the path of life's storms.

It is possible not only to survive in a crisis, but actually to thrive on it. No better example exists than in the person of Dr. Stephen Hawking, a thirty-seven-year-old astrophysicist at the University of Cambridge in England. He is generally believed to be the most brilliant scientist since Einstein, and certainly, the most gifted theoretical astronomer now living. What may not be known, however, is that Dr. Hawking has a progressive neuromuscular disease called amyotrophic lateral sclerosis. (ALS is the disease that took the life of Yankee baseball player Lou Gehrig.) Hawking is confined to a wheelchair and is barely able to move his arms or legs. His body has now deteriorated to where he can speak only with the greatest effort. His attempts to communicate have become so labored that those who don't know him think he has expressed an entire thought, when in fact, he's only spoken a few words. He is too weak to write, feed himself, comb his hair, or fix his glasses. *Omni Magazine* said this about him: "Hawking . . . can do little but sit and think. His mind is a blackboard. He memorizes the long strings of equations that give life to his ideas, then dictates the results to his colleagues or secretary—a feat that has been compared to Beethoven's writing an entire symphony in his head."

The article in *Omni Magazine* then quoted Dr. Hawking as he assessed his reaction to the illness. I can't forget his words. He said that before he was stricken with the disease, he was bored with his profession and with life in general. Nothing interested or motivated him. He drank too much and did little work. Then came the catastrophic illness and his attitudes changed dramatically. The privilege of living became especially precious to him. Speaking of this awakening, Dr. Hawking said, "When one's expectations [for life] are reduced to zero, one really appreciates everything that one does have."*

What a tremendous insight! The human emotional appatatus is constructed so as to disregard that which is taken for granted. Good health, delicious food, pleasant entertainment, peaceful circumstances, and beautiful homes are of little consequence to those who have had them since birth. Can you recall seeing a healthy teenager get up in the morning and express appreciation because his joints didn't hurt, or his vision was excellent, or because he breathed with ease or he felt so good? Not likely. He has never known the meaning of prolonged pain or sickness, and he accepts his good health without even considering it. But when those greatest of life's blessings begin to vanish, our appreciation for them increases accordingly. For a man like Stephen Hawking, who now faces continued physical deterioration and premature death, the whole world assumes new significance: the beauty of a tree, the privilege of watching a sunset, the company of loved ones—it all takes on meaning.

Let's apply this concept to the American way of life, which will explain many of the emotional problems and psychiatric symptoms which beset us. We have been taught to anticipate the finest and best from our existence on this earth. We feel almost entitled, by divine decree, to at least seventy-two years of bliss, and anything less than that is a cause for great agitation. In other words, our *level of expectation* is incredibly high. But life rarely delivers on that promise. It deals us disappointment and frustration and disease and pain and loneliness, even in the best of circumstances. Thus, there is an inevitable gap between life as it *is* and life as it ought to be.

The result is a high incidence of depression, especially among

---

*Dennis Overbye, *Omni Magazine*, February 1979, p. 46.

women, and an unacceptable rate of suicide, especially among the young, and a general anxiety among the rest of us. I have watched men develop ulcers over relatively insignificant business reverses. I have seen women suffer daily agitation over the most minor inconveniences, such as having too small a house or a cranky neighbor, when every other dimension of their lives was without a blemish.

Compare the instability of such individuals with the attitudes of German families near the close of World War II. Every night, a thousand British bombers would unload their destructive cargo over Hamburg and Berlin and Munich. By day, the American planes would do the same. Loved ones were dying on all sides. Neighborhoods were shattered and burned. Little children were maimed and killed. There was not enough food to eat and the water was polluted. The fabric of their lives was shredded. Yet historians tell us that their morale remained intact until the end of the war. They did not crack. They went about the business of reordering their homes and making the best of a horrible situation.

How can we account for this courage in the face of disaster, as compared with affluent Americans who, though they have everything, are wringing their hands in the offices of psychiatrists? The difference, in the words of Stephen Hawking, is in our level of expectations. The Germans expected to sacrifice and experience suffering. They were, therefore, prepared for the worst when it came. But we are vulnerable to the slightest frustration, because we have been taught that troubles could be avoided. We have permitted our emotions to rule us, and in so doing, we have become mere slaves to our feelings.

Even Christian ministers have contributed to this distortion. "Become a follower of Christ and end your troubles," goes the sales pitch. "You can prosper in your business . . . and, in fact, if you'll utter the right noises to God, He'll make you rich. You can avoid all sickness and all injury and all physical malfunctions." It's quite a package, when you think about it.

Unfortunately, the promise is unscriptural. Jesus said, "In the world, ye *shall* have tribulation: but be of good cheer; I have overcome the world" (John 16:33, KJV, emphasis added).

Christianity has always been *future*-oriented. "And God shall wipe away all tears from their eyes; and there shall be no more death, neither sorrow, nor crying, neither shall there be any more pain: for the former things are passed away" (Rev. 21:4, KJV). Nowhere does the Bible promise such ease and bliss in this life, however. In fact, the Scripture indicates just the opposite— that trials are sent our way so that we can grow and become stronger. Those who hold tenaciously to the other point of view—that God is obligated to remove every source of stress— must explain why He permitted John the Baptist to be falsely accused and beheaded, and why the Apostle Paul spent so much time in dungeons. They must also interpret the following Scripture written in Hebrews 11:35–39, TLB:

> But others trusted God and were beaten to death, preferring to die rather than turn from God and be free—trusting that they would rise to a better life afterwards.
>
> Some were laughed at and their backs cut open with whips, and others were chained in dungeons. Some died by stoning and some by being sawed in two; others were promised freedom if they would renounce their faith, then were killed with the sword. Some went about in skins of sheep and goats, wandering over deserts and mountains, hiding in dens and caves. They were hungry and sick and ill-treated—too good for this world. And these men of faith, though they trusted God and won his approval, none of them received all that God had promised them.

I am reminded of Job, in the Old Testament, who lost all his possessions and his children. Then his health deteriorated. There he was, sitting on the ground, covered with boils, lonely for his family, impoverished, rejected by his friends, and wondering whatever happened to God. But in that hour of blackness when every imaginable misfortune had befallen him, his faith did not falter. His spirit did not break. Instead, he looked upward from his misery and said, "Though he slay me, yet will I trust in him" (Job 13:15, KJV). That, for all times, is the classic example of a man's intellect and his will refusing to capitulate to emotion and circumstances.

Summary

Much has been written about the need for men to get in touch with their feelings—to be willing (and able) to cry and love and hope. These suggestions are valid. As we will see in a subsequent chapter, my father, who symbolized masculinity for me, was a very tender man who was not ashamed to weep. I certainly am not suggesting that men display a Crest-test cheerfulness when they are dying inside. Nevertheless, there are dangers in permitting emotions to rule our minds. Feelings must not dominate rational judgment, especially in times of crisis, nor should we allow the minor frustrations of living to produce depression and despair.

Though I hope never to experience the measure of sorrow suffered by Job and the Biblical martyrs, I want to adopt their steadfastness when trouble comes my way. Likewise, as the head of my family, I want to lower our level of expectations in anticipation of the winter. As Dr. Hawking indicated, life will take on new meaning if we are successful in that endeavor.

Footprints

One night a man had a dream. He dreamed he was walking along the beach with the Lord. Across the sky flashed scenes from his life. For each scene, he noticed two sets of footprints in the sand: one belonging to him, and the other to the Lord.

191

When the last scene of his life flashed before him, he looked back at the footprints in the sand. He noticed that many times along the path of his life there was only one set of footprints. He also noticed that it happened at the very lowest and saddest times in his life.

This really bothered him and he questioned the Lord about it. "Lord, you said that once I decided to follow you, you'd walk with me all the way. But I have noticed that during the most troublesome times in my life, there is only one set of footprints. I don't understand why when I needed you most you would leave me."

The Lord replied, "My son, my precious child, I love you and I would never leave you. During your times of trial and suffering, when you see only one set of footprints, it was then that I carried you."

Author unknown

Chapter 16

A Man and His Animals

SHOW ME HOW a man treats his animals, and I'll show you what he thinks of people." That's a proverb with numerous exceptions, of course, but a correlation does exist. Anyone who would care about the welfare of a helpless dog or cat or bird is likely to have a soft spot for hurting people, as well. My dad was such a man. He loved everything God made, especially furry little canines called toy terriers.

Penny was a brilliant representative of that breed. We adopted him into our family when I was thirteen years of age, and the two of us grew up together. By the time I left for college, he was established as a full-fledged member of the Dobson household, with all the rights and privileges thereof. He and my dad had a special understanding for one another, like two old friends who could communicate deep feelings without uttering a word. Only dog lovers will fully comprehend what I mean.

But alas, Penny grew old and decrepit. At seventeen years of age, he was afflicted with a terminal case of cancer and was obviously experiencing severe pain. He would walk the fence and moan hour after hour. My dad knew the time had come to put his little friend to sleep, but he couldn't bring himself to do it.

"How can I kill my dog?" he would ask.

But it was more cruel to let Penny suffer. So Dad made an appointment with the veterinarian at the humane society to discuss the matter. The doctor was a perceptive man and recognized how painful this event was for my father. He shared a similar situation with reference to his own dog, and these two grown men sat and wept together.

The decision was made to end Penny's life, and the day was chosen. Throughout the prior afternoon, a man and a dog sat together under the vine-covered arbor in their back yard. Neither spoke. (Penny communicated his thoughts with his ears and eyes and tail.) I suspect they both cried. Then they said goodbye for the final time.

When the moment came, Penny was given five barbiturates to prevent him from recognizing the despised smell of the kennel. My mother handed him to the attendant and then hurried back to the car. Dad was visibly shaken. For nearly a week, he sat alone under the arbor, going there immediately after fulfilling his teaching responsibilities at the college each day. He continued to grieve for Penny for several years.

During this time, we encouraged my father to get another dog, but he was reluctant to expose himself to another painful loss. Nine years passed before he considered trying to replace the memory of Penny.

But wait, why don't I let him tell you the story in his own words. The following narrative was written by my dad, shortly before his death.

Guaranteed Healthy

I like dogs. Some of my best friends are dogs! I sometimes think
that I can communicate better with dogs than I can with people. At
least I have never had a dog misunderstand me to the point of
breaking up a friendship once it was established! I had grieved for
my little toy terrier, Penny, for nine years. I said I would never get
another dog. Some of this was due to the Judas Iscariot kind of guilt
I was carrying. You see, I was forced by my very love for him to end
his hopeless agony. I, his trusted keeper, betrayed him to his
executioner! Penny, so gentle, so obedient, so intelligent! Gone was
my constant companion of seventeen years! I miss him still and
always will but "Nine years is enough," I told my wife. "I will get me
another dog."

"You are just asking for more pain," she said. "A dog's life usually
averages about eight to ten years—then you will have to go through
this sorrow again."

"Maybe not," I said. "I have thought a lot about this decision. I
will soon be over the hill myself. It could be that we will arrive at
the Golden Gate at about the same time."

I decided to take great care in selecting this new pet. I wanted the
same kind of dog, a toy terrier, but he would have to be pedigreed.
Penny had been a lucky accident—a throw-back more like his fox
terrier ancestors. I know the breed and know, too, that beyond the
A.K.C. papers, you have to select the individual dog for intelligence and other desirable qualities. You have to get a pup by six
weeks of age, to be sure he hasn't been ruined by someone else.
Then he would have to be in perfect health, having had the
necessary shots, etc.

All these thoughts were getting settled in my mind as I started
watching the papers for dog advertisements. No luck. Someone
would always beat me to the best dogs, since I wouldn't answer an ad
on Sunday, and that's when thoroughbreds were offered. Finally, I
saw a notice from a pet shop about a toy terrier, but I didn't take it
seriously.

"There's something funny about this," I told my wife. "The ad
says the dog is a nine-month-old thoroughbred, but he has no

papers. Nine months in a pet shop and nobody wants him! It doesn't sound good to me. I wouldn't buy an unregistered dog anyway!" But later, I said, "Let's just drive out and see him."

We found the shop in a run-down section of the city. My wife was almost afraid to get out of the car. The business was in one room of an old abandoned house. When I stepped through the front door, the stench almost overwhelmed me. I spotted the dog in question at once. He was crowded into a cubicle with other larger puppies who were bumping him and stepping on his tiny body. They were a motley assortment of mongrels of various kinds, all yapping and defecating; some were trying to sleep away their misery, curled up on the wire bottom of their filthy enclosure!

When the saleslady brought the little toy terrier out and put him down on the floor he seemed to be in a wall-eyed trance.

"This dog has been through some traumatic emotional experience," I thought. He looked up at me with pitiful glazed eyes that reflected unspeakable sadness. Far from considering him, I couldn't believe anyone would offer an animal for sale in this condition. His skinny little frame, all four pounds of it, was trembling, and every few seconds he would cough and gag from some kind of chest infection. I thought I recognized this as a case of the dreaded distemper. Between coughs, he would dig frantically at his ears, which were infested with mites. He would follow me about the room, meekly, his tiny tail clamped tightly down—a picture of dejection.

"Nobody knows what other disease he has got—maybe incurable," I thought. "Oh, no! I'm not getting into that!" But in spite of myself I wanted to cry. He seemed to be saying, "You look like a nice man, but I know you will be like all the rest." He was so little and helpless and hopeless. While I was hardening myself to his unhappy fate with such reasoning as "It's not my fault . . . I can't turn my home into a dog hospital," he put out his warm pink tongue and licked my hand, as much to say, "Thanks, anyway, for coming to see me." I had to get out of there quick!

We were silent as we drove away. When we had gone a few blocks I made an instant decision. I guess it was the effect of that lick on the hand—the intuitive longing it expressed! Wheeling the car around, I started back. I turned stone deaf to the neatly logical reasoning my wife poured into my ear. In a split second, instead of a nameless wart of a dog in a rotten pet shop, that had become my little dog in there, suffering and lonely and sick! I was bursting with compassion that should rightfully have been expended on a more worthy object: I know, God, please forgive me. I wrote the check and received in exchange a receipt for the money. On it were the incredible words, *"Guaranteed Healthy!"*

I folded the shivering form into my arms, stink and all. A warm bath soon removed the nauseating smell; then I took him to the best veterinarian I could find. He took one look and shook his head.

"I'll try, but I can't promise he will make it," he said. It was days of antibiotics for the cough, weeks of application of drops for the ear mites, worm medicine, shots of various kinds, a tonic to regulate that wildly beating little heart, and love made warm and tender by years of grieving for Penny. And to the astonishment of the doctor, most of all, we have a dog to be proud of, fit and sound.

And talk about gratitude! My pup, whom we named Benji, expresses it in the blasphemous, idolatrous way he worships me. He thinks I am God Almighty when he comes to meet me in the morning, twisting and wiggling like he will tear himself in two. It is as though he will never allow himself to forget his private hell in the pet shop!

Three years after this happy beginning, Benji was to lose his beloved master. He had seen my mother and father leave in the car one morning, but only one of them returned. No one could explain to him the meaning of death, of course. So Benji sat waiting month in and out, straining to hear the sound of that familiar voice. The shutting of a car door would bring him hope and excitement . . . followed by obvious disappointment. Wrong person, again.

I visited my mother several months after the funeral to help pack my father's possessions and give away his clothes. As I busily folded coats and pants and placed them in a suitcase, Benji jumped on the bed. He reverently approached the clothes and sniffed them carefully on all sides. He climbed into the suitcase and curled up within one of my father's most familiar coats. Then he looked up at me.

"I understand, Benji. I miss him, too," I said.

Conclusion

Why have I included a story about a dog in a book about men? I guess I wanted to illustrate that husbands and fathers are entitled to feel and love and enjoy. Those like my father who can permit themselves the experience of deep emotions are much more vulnerable to the vicissitudes of life, admittedly, but their sensitivity is worth the price they pay for it.

SECTION VII

A MAN AND HIS GOD

Chapter 17

A Man and His God

ONE OF MY colleagues died a few weeks ago, having served on our university medical faculty for more than twenty-five years. During his tenure as a professor, he had earned the respect and admiration of both professionals and patients, especially for his research findings and contribution to medical knowledge. This doctor had reached the pinnacle of success in his chosen field, and enjoyed the status and financial rewards that accompany such accomplishment. He had tasted every good thing, by the standards of the world.

At the next staff meeting following his death, a five-minute eulogy was read by a member of his department. Then the chairman invited the entire staff to stand, as is our custom in situations of this nature, for one minute of silence in memory of the fallen colleague. I have no idea what the other members of the staff contemplated during that sixty-second pause, but I can tell you what was going through my mind.

I was thinking, "Lord, is this what it all comes down to? We sweat and worry and labor to achieve a place in life, to impress our fellow men with our competence. We take ourselves so seriously, overreacting to the insignificant events of each passing day. Then finally, even for the brightest among us, all these experiences fade into history and our lives are summarized with a five-minute eulogy and sixty seconds of silence. It hardly seems worth the effort, Lord."

But I was also struck by the collective inadequacy of that faculty to deal with the questions raised by our friend's death. Where had he gone? Would he live again? Will we see him on the other side? Why was he born? Were his deeds observed and recorded by a loving God? Is that God interested in *me*? Is there meaning to life beyond investigative research and professorships and expensive automobiles? The silent response by two hundred and fifty learned men and women seemed to symbolize our inability to cope with these issues.

Then a wave of relief spread over me as I thought about the message of Christianity and the meaning of the cross. This Good News provides the *only* satisfactory explanation for why we're here and where we're going. The final heartbeat for the Christian is not the mysterious conclusion to a meaningless existence. It is, rather, the grand beginning to a life that will never end. That's why we can proclaim, even at the graveside of a loved one, "O death, where is thy sting? O grave, where is thy victory?" (1 Cor. 15:55, KJV).

How extremely important it is for the man of the home to know the answers to these perplexing questions, and be able to lead his family in the paths of righteousness. When he accepts that spiritual responsibility as God intends, the entire family is likely to follow his example. "And they said, Believe on the Lord, Jesus Christ, and thou shalt be saved, *and thy house*" (Acts 16:31, KJV, emphasis added). This issue is of such significance

202

that I feel compelled to devote the balance of this chapter to the basic plan of salvation. Perhaps someone will comprehend the Christian message for the first time through reading these pages, which is my prayer.

I used to ponder a difficult theological question that appeared unanswerable at the time. It seemed strange that God would send His only Son, Jesus, to die in agony on the cross at Mount Calvary. I reasoned that God, as Creator of the universe, was in charge of everything. That entitled Him to make His own rules and establish His own boundaries. Therefore, it seemed to me that God could have provided *any* plan of salvation He chose—anything that suited His fancy.

It was illogical that God would create a system that would ultimately require the suffering and death of His own Son on the cross. I could not comprehend why He would put Himself through such grief and sorrows on our behalf when He could have offered a less costly plan of salvation. I struggled with this issue as a young Christian and was perplexed by the questions it raised. I knew all the pat answers given to me in Sunday school, and I could quote the Scriptures. But none of the interpretations satisfied me.

It is interesting to look back on the things that troubled us in earlier days. I now have a better understanding of God's plan of salvation and what motivated it. And the explanation is of great significance for me, because it deals with the very essence of Christianity.

Before reading my conclusion about God's plan, you should know that I am neither a minister nor a pastor nor a theologian. I can make no claims to theological expertise. I do, however, know a little Greek and a little Hebrew. The Greek owns a gas station in Los Angeles, and the Hebrew runs a delicatessen in San Diego. That's a very bad joke, but it illustrates the fact that I am admittedly unqualified to speak as a Biblical authority. However, this lack of theological sophistication may prove to be an advantage in that it will make it easier for me to communicate my thoughts in common, everyday terms. (Theologians prefer to use no words with fewer than 12 letters.) If my explanation becomes a gross oversimplification for some people, I hope they'll forgive me.

Here, then, is my concept of the plan of salvation and why Jesus' death was necessary: It begins, as it should, with an understanding of God's nature. Throughout Scripture, the Almighty is represented by two uncompromising characteristics: *his love and His justice.* Both of these aspects are reflected in everything God does, and none of His actions will ever contradict either component.

The love and justice of God were especially evident when He created Adam and Eve. Obviously, He could have "programmed" them to love Him and obey His laws. This could have been accomplished by creating them as highly sophisticated robots or puppets. He did, in fact, program the brains of lower animals, causing birds to build a certain kind of nest and wolves to kill wounded elk. They have no choice in the matter. My Dachshund, Siggie, displays an assortment of wired-in behavior about which *neither* of us has a choice. For example, he can't help barking when the front doorbell rings, even if I threaten to kill him for waking the baby. Nor can he keep from gobbling his food as though he would never get another meal. God has imposed instinctual behavior in Siggie (some of which I would like to eliminate) which operates automatically and without learning.

But the Lord elected to put no instinctual behavior in mankind, leaving us free to learn. This explains the utter helplessness of human infants, who are the most dependent of all creatures at birth. They lack the initial advantages of unlearned responses but will later run circles around the brightest animals with "locked-in" reactions. Such is the nature of our humanness.

By granting us freedom of choice, therefore, God gave meaning to our love. He sought our devotion but refused to demand it. However, the moment He created this choice, it became inevitable that He would eventually be faced with man's sin. I've heard Christians speculate on what might have happened if Adam and Eve hadn't disobeyed God. The answer is obvious. If they had not sinned, a subsequent generation would have. After all, if no one ever made the wrong choice, then there was no true choice to be made.

But Adam and Eve *did* sin, as we know, and thereby confronted God with the most serious dilemma of all time. His love for the human race was unlimited, which required that He forgive His disobedient children. The Bible says, "As a father pitieth his children, so the Lord pitieth them that fear him" (Ps. 103:13, KJV). That is an analogy I can comprehend. I know how I pity my children when they've done wrong. My inclination is to forgive them.

But in spite of God's great love, His justice required complete obedience. It demanded repentance and punishment for disobedience. So herein was a serious conflict with God's nature. If He destroyed the human race, as His justice would require in response to our sinful disobedience, His love would have been violated: but if He ignored our sins, His justice would have been sacrificed. Yet neither aspect of His nature could be compromised.

But God, in His marvelous wisdom, proposed a solution to that awful dilemma. If he could find one human being who wasn't worthy of damnation—just one individual in the history of mankind who had never sinned, a man or a woman who was not guilty—then the sin of every other person on earth could be laid upon that one and He could suffer for all of us. So God, being timeless, looked across the ages of man from Adam to Armageddon, but He could not find anyone who was innocent. "For all have sinned, and come short of the glory of God" (Rom. 3:23, KJV) it would later be written. There wasn't a person who was worthy of assuming the guilt, blame, and punishment for the rest of us. Therefore, the only alternative was for God to send His own Son to bear the sins of the entire human family. And herein we see the beauty of God's plan and the reason Jesus had to die. When He was crucified here on earth, Jesus harmonized the conflict between God's love and justice and provided a remedy for fallen mankind.

Thus, Jesus said as He was dying, "It is finished!" meaning, "I have carried out the plan of salvation that God designed for sinful man." And that's why God turned His back on Jesus when He was on the cross, prompting Him to cry in anguish, "My God, my God, why hast thou forsaken me?" (Matt. 27:46, KJV). In that moment, Jesus was bearing the punishment for all human sins down through the ages, including yours and mine.

This understanding of the plan of salvation is not based on guesses and suppositions, of course. It is drawn from the literal interpretation of God's Word. This message is, in fact, the primary theme of all Scripture. The Old Testament says, "Jesus is coming!" and the New Testament proclaims, "Jesus is here!" But if I had to select one passage to represent the concept I've presented, it would be the 53rd chapter of Isaiah (my favorite chapter in the Bible). It was written seven hundred years before the birth of Christ and provides an incredible prophecy of His mission. The summary of God's entire plan is presented in this one chapter. Let me quote it from *The Living Bible:*

But oh, how few will believe it! Who will listen? To whom will God reveal his saving power? In God's eyes he was like a tender green shoot, sprouting from a root in dry and sterile ground. But in our eyes there was no attractiveness at all, nothing to make us want him. We despised him and rejected him—a man of sorrows, acquainted with bitterest grief. We turned our backs on him and looked the other way when he went by. He was despised and we didn't care.

Yet it was *our* grief he bore, *our* sorrows that weighed him down. And we thought his troubles were a punishment from God, for his *own* sins! But he was wounded and bruised for *our* sins. He was chastised that we might have peace; he was lashed—and we were

206

healed! *We* are the ones who strayed away like sheep! *We,* who left God's paths to follow our own. Yet God laid on *him* the guilt and sins of every one of us!

He was oppressed and he was afflicted, yet he never said a word. He was brought as a lamb to the slaughter; and as a sheep before her shearers is dumb, so he stood silent before the ones condemning him. From prison and trial they led him away to his death. But who among the people of that day realized it was their sins that he was dying for—that he was suffering their punishment? He was buried like a criminal in a rich man's grave; but he had done no wrong, and had never spoken an evil word.

Yet it was the Lord's good plan to bruise him and fill him with grief. But when his soul has been made an offering for sin, then he shall have a multitude of children, many heirs. He shall live again and God's program shall prosper in his hands. And when he sees all that is accomplished by the anguish of his soul, he shall be satisfied; and because of what he has experienced, my righteous Servant shall make many to be counted righteous before God, for he shall bear all their sins. Therefore I will give him the honors of one who is mighty and great, because he has poured out his soul unto death. He was counted as a sinner, and he bore the sins of many, and he pled with God for sinners (Isa. 53, TLB).

Isn't that a beautiful explanation of Jesus' purpose here on earth? It makes clear why God's plan necessarily involved His own Son—His grief and sorrow and death. Only by paying this incredible price could He harmonize the potential contradiction between love and justice, and provide a "way of escape" for mankind. It also explains why there is no other name by which we are saved and why we cannot escape if we neglect so great a salvation (Heb. 2:3).

One important question remains to be answered: Just how does a person proceed, now, to accept this plan and follow the risen Lord? I believe there are two basic steps in that process (although some churches emphasize only one). The first is to believe in the name of Jesus Christ. John 3:16 (KJV) says, "For

207

God so loved the world, that he gave his only begotten Son, that whosoever believeth in him should not perish, but have everlasting life." Romans 10:13 (TLB) says it another way: "Anyone who calls upon the name of the Lord will be saved." So the first obligation for anyone is to accept what Christ did as being for him, personally.

But as I understand the Scripture, and from my own theological perspective, there's a second responsibility which is often underemphasized. James expressed it like this: "Are there still some among you who hold that 'only believing' is enough? Believing in one God? Well, remember that the demons believe this too—so strongly that they tremble in terror! When will you ever learn that 'believing' is useless without *doing* what God wants you to do? Faith that does not result in good deeds is not real faith" (2:19, TLB). So something else is required. While it's true that you can't "work" your way into salvation—you cannot do enough good deeds to earn it—*repentance* is still an important part of the process.

"Repentance" is a word that's often misunderstood. What does it really mean? Billy Graham defined repentance as having three parts to it. The first is conviction. You have to know what is right before you can do what is right; and you have to know what is wrong in order to avoid those misbehaviors. Repentance also involves a deep awareness that you stand guilty before the Lord. I've seen people who call themselves Christians and say, "Yes, I believe in Jesus," but they seem to have no real comprehension or awareness of their own sin and guilt. They have no "contriteness" of heart. From the Scripture in James we see that even demons "believe and tremble"; yet *many individuals believe and do not tremble.*

But where does this spirit of repentance originate? It must come through the teaching of the Holy Spirit. Deuteronomy 4:29 says, "But if from thence [from this point forward] thou shalt seek the Lord thy God, thou shalt find him, if thou seek him with all thy heart and with all thy soul" (KJV). So you must want this relationship with God. He must be so important that you will allow Him to turn your life around and change your behavior. In summary, then, repentance includes conviction, knowing right from wrong; then contrition, being aware of your guilt and sin; and finally, a resulting change of mind and heart and behavior.

Time and space limitations make it impossible to discuss other important theological issues of relevance to salvation, including *confession* (Rom. 10:9–10) and *baptism* (Acts 22:16 and 2:38). Entire volumes have been written on a topic I have attempted to address in a single chapter. Perhaps I have, at least, provided a foundation from which the reader can launch his own study of the Bible.

I think it would be helpful, in conclusion, to give an example of the kind of prayer that a person might pray if he understands what I've been writing and wants to accept Jesus Christ as his own Lord and Savior. Let me express it in this way:

Lord, I bring you my sinful nature as you've revealed it to me. I know I don't have anything valuable to offer except myself and my love. I can't earn your forgiveness but you've offered it as a free gift from your Son, Jesus Christ. I accept your control of my life, and intend to serve You, obey You and follow You from this moment forward. You have my past, my present, my future, my family, my money and my time. *Nothing* will I withhold. Thank you for loving me and forgiving me and making me your own. Amen.

Sanctuary

Through the mesquite brush in the evening hush
   Down a road that is dimly described
Past the dead cow's bones and the blackened stones
   Where the ghost of an Indian hides

Straight Talk to Men and Their Wives

Like a wild thing to drink at the windmill tank
    Winds the trail now disguised of intent
Down the dry gulch bed to the rise up ahead
    Where the wolf seeks the jackrabbit's scent

Yonder beck'ning spire is the windmill's tower
    Far away in the shimmering haze
Both cathedral and shrine is this derrick of mine
    Like my heart, lifting high, full of praise

See those galloping steeds, the tumbleweeds
    How they fret 'neath the barbed wire fence
Fastly hitched for this hour, they are shorn of their power
    Till the night wind shall call them hence.

Heaven's vesper song seems to call me along
    Through the purple and violet and blue
Congregation of one, to my God I have come
    And the top of this tower is my pew

Up the weathered flank on the ladder's plank
    To my perch near the wheel and the vane
Nor regret that my rest's taken hard by the nest
    Of the hawk circling wide o'er the plain

Now the mill's rumbling throat yields a pipe-organ note
    Though some say it creaks and it scolds
To the wheel's waving palms, there's a giving of alms
    As the sun turns the green into gold

Limpid waters outspill, with a lyrical rill
    From the rusty old pipes down below
And my soul stands enawed, for the presence of God
    Heavy rides on the evening glow

James C. Dobson, Sr.

Chapter 18

A Man and His Death

"An infant is born with a clenched fist, but an old man dies with an open hand. Life has a way of prying loose our grasp on all that seems so important."

How DOES A good man die? We are given numerous examples in the Scriptures which serve as inspiration to those who call themselves Christians. My favorite is the account of King David's final hours, when he asked that his beloved son Solomon be brought to his chambers. There, in the presence of witnesses, a father offered his concluding words of advice to the young man he had designated to succeed him. We can be certain that the statements made on that occasion carried great significance, for David was obviously conveying eternal truths to his son. A man is seldom casual or frivolous when staring death

211

in the face. Thus, these words represent a summation of all that David believed and loved:

> And thou, Solomon my son, *know thou the God of thy father,* and serve him with a perfect heart and with a willing mind: for the Lord searcheth all hearts, and understandeth all the imaginations of the thoughts: *if thou seek him, he will be found of thee; but if thou forsake him, he will cast thee off forever* (1 Chron. 28:9, KJV, emphasis added).

Every son should be so fortunate as to receive such profound advice from his father. Those sixty words contain all that a young man or woman should know to live a successful and meaningful life. Notice the precision of David's words. He did not instruct Solomon to get.to know *about* God. He told him to become acquainted directly *with* God. The distinction is vital (I may know *about* Jimmy Carter and George Washington and Albert Einstein but I have never met them face to face). I am also impressed by David's reference to God's judgment for those who disobey His commandments: "But if thou forsake Him, He will cast thee off forever." That warning has eternal implications for you and me, as well.

We've seen how King David approached the benediction of his life on earth. Let me, now, offer a more contemporary example of how a good man dies. It is fitting that I devote these concluding words to my own father. He provided the inspiration for the entire book, as you must know by this point.

The last chapter in the life of my dad begins at Eastertime 1977, when my parents came to visit Shirley and me in California. I took several days off work and spent that time in pleasant conversation with our loved ones. At one point, I turned to my dad and asked spontaneously, "What do you want for an epitaph at the close of your life?"

He thought briefly and then replied, "Only two words: 'He prayed.'" I can think of no phrase that better summarized his devotion to God and the daily communion he maintained with

Him. It is fitting that his final act on earth was to ask for God's blessing on the meal that had been prepared. Accordingly, those two words, "He prayed," appear on his footstone today.

I then turned to my mother and asked, "What epitaph do you want on your tombstone?" She has a rich sense of humor and immediately responded, "I told you I was sick!"

Her remark reminded me of the eighty-year-old man who said, "If I'd have known I was gonna live so long I'd have taken better care of myself!"

We enjoyed that week of laughter and fellowship with my parents, having no idea, of course, that this was to be the last trip my father would take. The clock was ticking down toward zero, with only eight months remaining.

Later in the year, as death approached, my dad was to experience two concluding revelations from God that moved him deeply. I learned about the first in a telephone conversation in September. We were talking about my upcoming television series and various topics of mutual interest. Then suddenly Dad said, "Well, there's one thing I know. God is going to take care of your mother."

I replied, "Yes, I'm sure He will," but wondered why he had chosen that occasion to make such a statement. Five days later, he suffered his near-fatal heart attack.

As my mother and I sat in the hospital waiting for news of his progress, I remembered his strange comment on the telephone. I shared his words with my mother and asked if she understood why he had chosen to tell me about her secure future.

"I know what he meant," she replied. She then told me that two weeks earlier, my dad had been resting on the bed while she worked around the room. She glanced at him and noticed that there were tears in his eyes.

"What's the matter?" she asked.

He paused for a few seconds and then said, "The Lord just spoke to me."

"Do you want to tell me about it?" she continued.

"It was about you!" replied my dad.

"Then you'd *better* tell me!" she said.

"It was a strange experience," said my dad. "I was just lying here thinking about many things. I wasn't praying or even thinking about you when the Lord spoke to me and said, 'I'm going to take care of Myrtle.'" They looked at each other in awe, wondering what it meant.

Five days later, they experienced the most severe trauma of their lives, and eighty-four days hence, my mother learned the meaning of widowhood.

Although many months have passed since the death of my father on that cold December day, the Lord's promise has not been forgotten. I won't impose all the details on you. Let it simply be known that the God of my father has comforted, provided for, and sustained the woman he left behind.

Of course, she still grieves for the man she loved. There is *no* painless way to lose a constant companion and friend of forty-three years. The early evening hours are especially lonely, and my mother has used them to write poetry to the memory of her husband. I especially appreciated the following piece which she permitted me to share with you:

I Thought I Saw You Today

I thought I saw you today.
Standing with your hands in your pockets.
Laughing, the wind playing mischievously
    with your hair.
My heart lunged toward you as
You disappeared, leaving a total stranger
    standing there.
How could I have imagined the
    man to be my darling . . .
My precious darling.

—Myrtle Dobson

It is the nature of things that *most* married women will eventually become widows. Thus, I'm sure that millions of women would understand perfectly the heartache my mother was conveying with these brief words.

I learned of my dad's second revelation on October 2, 1977, after he had been hospitalized for two weeks. I flew to Kansas City for a brief visit, which was to be the final time I would see him alive. He was brimming over with effervescence on that Sunday morning. He had so much he wanted to say to me. His medical progress appeared encouraging and he was anticipating being released from the hospital in a few days. Among weightier subjects, we discussed his little dog, Benji, who anxiously awaited the return of his master.

Then my dad became very serious. "There's something I want to try to describe to you," he said. "I had the most incredible experience the morning after my heart attack." He began weeping as he spoke.

I was concerned that his emotional state would affect his heart, and I asked him to wait and tell me later. He agreed and we let the matter drop. I had to leave the following day, and he died before our planned rendezvous at Christmas.

My dad did reveal the details of his experience to my mother and to a friend, Dr. Dean Baldwin, the week prior to his death. Furthermore, in going through his writings after death, I discovered a partially completed description of the event, in his own handwriting. The narrative that follows was taken from those three sources, describing a dramatic vision that he saw the morning after his heart attack. (Remember that his physicians had predicted he wouldn't live through that night.) These are his approximate words.

"It happened in the early morning hours when I was neither awake nor asleep. I was lying there in my quiet hospital room, when I suddenly saw the most beautiful person I'd ever seen. His identity was not immeditaely revealed, but I now believe Him to have been Jesus. This was no dream, in the classic sense. I was conscious of my circumstances, and the figure was extremely vivid. It was apparent that I was being permitted to observe a kind of courtroom scene—a divine proceeding—but my being there was as an onlooker. No word was addressed to me directly. The 'person' was seated and he was writing in a book. It seemed that he was considering an extremely important issue. Then I realize it was *my* case he was evaluating. The details of my life were being reviewed carefully. He stopped writing and began to plead my case directly to God. I have never heard such eloquent language as he described my circumstances, calling me by name repeatedly. Then he continued to write until he came to the bottom of the page, at which time he completed the last sentence and thrust his hand outward in a sudden gesture. Though no words were spoken, his motion and his countenance revealed his conclusion about my life. It said, "For time and eternity, he is *acceptable!*"

Dr. Baldwin reports that my father was weeping openly as he described this dramatic experience. Then he explained, with great feeling, that he was given a concluding message of major significance, but it was too personal to disclose. He could not even reveal it to my mother, with whom he shared everything. We can only guess that his impending death was foreseen in that incredible moment.

The vision then disappeared, leaving my dad in the gray, early morning light of the hospital room. He was so deeply affected by the experience that he made no attempt to tell anyone about it until my visit two weeks later. Even to the time of his death, he couldn't talk of the matter without crying.

Some would claim that my dad experienced a drug-induced dream in that hour. I don't believe it. My father, who was not given to mystical exaggeration, was emphatic that the vision had not been a hallucination or imaginary event. I will leave it for the reader to decide. There is one fact, however, of which I am certain. This man *was* found "acceptable" by his Maker. He had lived by an uncompromising standard of devotion to Jesus

Christ. He had fought a good fight and kept the faith until the end.

The twenty-third Psalm promises the righteous that God will walk with them through the valley of the shadow of death. He certainly fulfilled that covenant on behalf of my father. And the life of this good man came to an end, only to continue in greater glory on the other side.

The passing of my dad has changed my own view of death. I still have an instinctual desire to live—especially since my work at home is incomplete—but I no longer perceive the end of life as the greatest of all tragedies. Now, I know I will be welcomed across the threshold by my old friend. I'm sure he will be so excited to show me the stars and planets and the heavenly city. I also expect him to introduce me, face to face, to the Lord I've tried to serve since I was three years old.

But for now, he is gone, and *I* am the one who is on trial in that divine courtroom. I am left with this prayer:

Heavenly Father, I yearn to be the kind of husband and father that you desire of me. My highest ideal on this earth is to earn those words of approval, "Well done, thou good and faithful servant." Yet I feel so inadequate to discharge my responsibility properly. I know that my children's concept of you will be greatly influenced by how they perceive me, and that thought is terrifying. But I know you only expect me to do the best I can, and that thought is comforting. Thank you for the model you gave me in my father. Help me now to perpetuate that example before the children whom you have loaned to Shirley and me. And though I've said it before, keep the circle unbroken when we stand before Your throne.

Finally, Lord, would you also give my dad a brief message for me. Tell him that I love him. No son ever owed his father more!

The drawing on the opposite page is by
Ray Craighead, a student of James Dobson, Sr.

JAMES DOBSON, SR.

1911–1977

"Yet we have this assurance: Those who belong to God shall live again. Their bodies shall rise again! Those who dwell in the dust shall awake and sing for joy! For God's light of life will fall like dew upon them!"—Isaiah 26:19, TLB

Other Materials for the Family
by Dr. James Dobson

BOOKS:

1. *Dare to Discipline*, Tyndale House Publishers, 1970. (Over one million copies of this text have been sold.)
2. *The Mentally Retarded Child and His Family*, Brunner-Mazel Publishers, 1970. (This book was co-edited with Dr. Richard Koch.)
3. *Hide or Seek*, Fleming H. Revell Company Publishers, 1974.
4. *What Wives Wish Their Husbands Knew About Women*, Tyndale House Publishers, 1975.
5. *The Strong-Willed Child*, Tyndale House Publishers, 1978.
6. *Preparing for Adolescence*, Vision House Publishers, 1978.

CASSETTE TAPE RECORDINGS:

1. *Discipline, Cradle to College*, Vision House Publishers (One Way Library). This album contains six cassette tapes, focusing on various aspects of discipline.
2. *Preparing for Adolescence*, Vision House Publishers (One Way Library). This album contains six cassette tapes, designed to help the pre-teenager prepare for the experience to come.
3. *Preparing for Adolescence Growth Pak*, Vision House Publishers and Word Publishers. Contains six cassette tapes for pre-teens, two tapes for parents and teachers, a workbook, a textbook and instruction sheets.
4. *Kids Need Self Esteem Too!* Vision House Publishers (One Way Library). This album contains six cassette tapes, and presents the ways parents and teachers can maximize self-confidence in children.
5. *What Wives Wish Their Husbands Knew About Women*, Vision House Publishers (One Way Library). This album deals with the basic content of the book by the same name although it contains speeches, radio interviews and counseling conversations.
6. *Focus on the Family*, Word Publishers. This twelve-tape album presents a panorama of topics relevant to family life, including marriage, parenthood, abortion, aging, family traditions, etc.

7. *Questions Parents Ask,* Word Publishers. This is a four-cassette album presenting more than sixty issues commonly raised by parents.

These and other items are available in local bookstores, or can be ordered by writing Focus on the Family, Box 952, Temple City, CA 91780. Dr. Dobson can also be contacted through that address, although he regrets that he is unable to respond to requests for personal consultation.